SHARED FOUNDATIONS

Explore

SHARED FOUNDATIONS SERIES

I. **INQUIRE,** by Lori Donovan

II. **INCLUDE,** by Julie Stivers

III. **COLLABORATE,** by Mary Catherine Coleman

IV. **CURATE,** by Len Bryan and Daniella Smith

V. **EXPLORE,** by Sarah Culp Searles

VI. **ENGAGE,** by Kathryn Roots Lewis and Marcia A. Mardis

SHARED FOUNDATIONS

Explore

SARAH CULP SEARLES

ALA Editions
CHICAGO | 2022

AASL
American Association
of School Librarians
TRANSFORMING LEARNING

ISBN: 978-0-8389-1919-4 (paper)

Library of Congress Cataloging-in-Publication Data

Names: Searles, Sarah Culp, 1985- author.
Title: Explore / Sarah Culp Searles.
Description: Chicago : ALA Editions, 2022. | Series: Shared foundations series ; V | Includes bibliographical references and index. | Summary: "This book offers a deeper understanding of the Explore Shared Foundation, including how to connect traditional practices while moving the school library profession forward; an examination of how the standards in Explore Shared Foundation relate to other major ideas and trends in school librarianship; and ready-to-implement programming for school librarians and those who support school librarians, including administrators, supervisors, and university educators"—Provided by publisher.
Identifiers: LCCN 2021001055 | ISBN 9780838919194 (paperback)
Subjects: LCSH: School libraries—Aims and objectives—United States. | School librarian participation in curriculum planning—United States. | Libraries and schools—United States.
Classification: LCC Z675.S3 S4175 2021 | DDC 027.80973—dc23
LC record available at https://lccn.loc.gov/2021001055

∞ This paper meets the requirements of ANSI/NISO Z39.48-1992 (Permanence of Paper).

Printed in the United States of America
26 25 24 23 22 5 4 3 2 1

Purchases of AASL publications and products fund advocacy, leadership, professional development, and standards initiatives for school librarians nationally.

ALA Editions purchases fund advocacy, awareness, and accreditation programs for library professionals worldwide.

SHARED FOUNDATION V

Explore

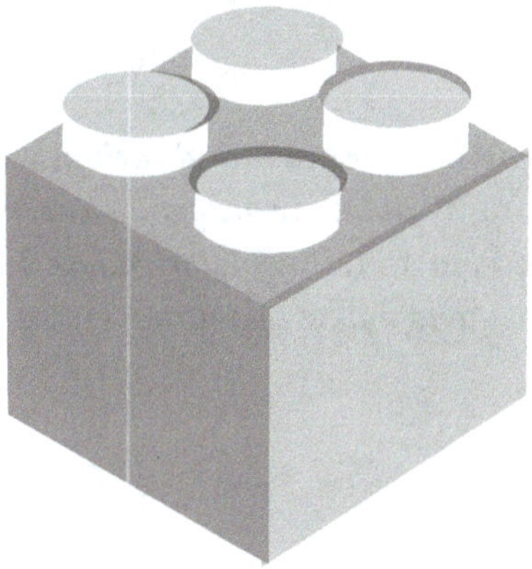

KEY COMMITMENT

Discover and innovate in a growth mindset developed through experience and reflection.

To Alan, my brave and curious explorer;
to William, my next great adventure;
and to Andy, my best friend and partner
who makes all journeys possible.

Contents

Acknowledgments

Any wisdom or insight that is now mine to share about school librarianship has been passed along by a lengthy chain of the educators, past and present, formal and informal, from whom I have been privileged to learn through exploration. I am indebted to countless colleagues in my state and national professional associations (the Tennessee Library Association, Tennessee Association of School Librarians, American Library Association, American Association of School Librarians, and the Lilead Project) for taking me under their wings when I was a young school librarian and helping me discover a bigger world. I am indebted to my many partners among the school leaders in the Knox County Schools, who consistently model reflective lifelong learning while welcoming me to the table for problem solving and design. I am indebted to the host of school librarians in my district who have trusted me as a collaborator and co-conspirator as we tinker and make creative new ways to serve learners. I am indebted to the university professors who taught me that I have a voice to contribute, and to the many personal and professional allies who've connected me with resources and experiences to inform that voice. And I am profoundly indebted to my family for teaching me that extraordinary things are done by ordinary people who show up, work hard with a growth mindset, and iterate. The greatest privilege and responsibility of exploration is to pay that learning forward to others.

Series Introduction

The Shared Foundations series from the American Association of School Librarians (AASL) examines the six Shared Foundations that anchor the comprehensive approach to teaching and learning in the *National School Library Standards for Learners, School Librarians, and School Libraries*. The Shared Foundations—Inquire, Include, Collaborate, Curate, Explore, and Engage—represent the core concepts that all learners, school librarians, and school libraries develop and promote in their K–12 learning environment.

Each of the six books in this series is dedicated to the deep exploration of a single Shared Foundation. Although each of the Shared Foundations supports its own inherent priorities, it cannot be implemented in isolation. The writing process used by the authors created a series of books that, like the AASL Standards Frameworks, are unique and yet parallel each other. Common elements are found throughout the series:

- A balance between theoretical discussion, practical strategies, and implementation examples, promoting reflection and creativity
- Development of the Competencies and Alignments for the Learner, School Librarian, and School Library in all four Domains—Think, Create, Share, and Grow
- Differences in application and assessment across grades K–12, promoting a growth mindset and envisioning outcomes for all learners, whether student learners, school librarians, or other educators
- An emphasis on personalized learning experiences, project-based learning, and authenticity of learning and projects
- Challenges addressed, illustrating ways to implement the Shared Foundations in various environments and levels of support

Questions for the Reflective Practitioner conclude each chapter, allowing readers to consider the application of concepts specific to their own learning communities and stimulate nuanced professional conversations. For ease of reference, readers also will find the AASL Standards Integrated Framework for the relevant Shared Foundation included in this work.

AASL and its series authors hope that this immersive and dedicated examination of the Shared Foundations will help school library professionals deepen their understandings, broaden their perspectives, make connections for personal relevance, and innovate and reflect on their practice with a professional community.

For more information about the *National School Library Standards*, and to access the latest implementation assistance resources, visit standards.aasl.org.

SHARED FOUNDATION V.

Explore

Domain	LEARNER DOMAINS AND COMPETENCIES	SCHOOL LIBRARIAN DOMAINS AND COMPETENCIES
A. Think	**Learners develop and satisfy personal curiosity by:** 1. Reading widely and deeply in multiple formats and write and create for a variety of purposes. 2. Reflecting and questioning assumptions and possible misconceptions. 3. Engaging in inquiry-based processes for personal growth.	**School librarians foster learners' personal curiosity by:** 1. Encouraging learners to read widely and deeply in multiple formats and write and create for a variety of purposes. 2. Challenging learners to reflect and question assumptions and possible misconceptions. 3. Enabling learners by helping them develop inquiry-based processes for personal growth.
B. Create	**Learners construct new knowledge by:** 1. Problem solving through cycles of design, implementation, and reflection. 2. Persisting through self-directed pursuits by tinkering and making.	**School librarians stimulate learners to construct new knowledge by:** 1. Teaching problem solving through cycles of design, implementation, and reflection. 2. Providing opportunities for tinkering and making. 3. Modeling persistence through self-directed tinkering and making.
C. Share	**Learners engage with the learning community by:** 1. Expressing curiosity about a topic of personal interest or curricular relevance. 2. Co-constructing innovative means of investigation. 3. Collaboratively identifying innovative solutions to a challenge or problem.	**School librarians prepare learners to engage with the learning community by:** 1. Providing strategies for acting on curiosity about a topic of personal interest or curricular relevance. 2. Assisting learners to co-construct innovative means of investigation. 3. Structuring activities for learners to collaboratively identify innovative solutions to a challenge or problem.
D. Grow	**Learners develop through experience and reflection by:** 1. Iteratively responding to challenges. 2. Recognizing capabilities and skills that can be developed, improved, and expanded. 3. Open-mindedly accepting feedback for positive and constructive growth.	**School librarians help learners develop through experience and reflection by:** 1. Scaffolding iterative challenge-response processes. 2. Helping learners to recognize capabilities and skills that can be developed, improved, and expanded. 3. Fostering an atmosphere in which constructive feedback is openly accepted for positive growth.

KEY COMMITMENT

Discover and innovate in a growth mindset developed through experience and reflection.

SCHOOL LIBRARY DOMAINS AND ALIGNMENTS — The school library facilitates the Key Commitment to and Competencies of EXPLORE	Domain
The school library supports learners' personal curiosity by: 1. Providing resources and strategies for inquiry-based processes. 2. Fostering opportunities for learners to demonstrate personal curiosity and creation of knowledge through engaging with a wide variety of resources and technology.	**A. Think**
The school library facilitates construction of new knowledge by: 1. Implementing technology as a tool or resource for learning. 2. Ensuring that multiple learning activities can occur in both physical and virtual spaces. 3. Establishing and maintaining a learning environment conducive to independent and collaborative exploration and problem solving.	**B. Create**
The school library prepares learners to engage with a larger learning community by: 1. Modeling and promoting the use of personal and professional learning networks. 2. Encouraging families and other members of the community to participate in school library activities. 3. Building and advocating for strong relationships with stakeholders who recognize and support an effective school library.	**C. Share**
The school library assists in the growth and development of learners by: 1. Leading other educators and learners to embrace a growth mindset through lifelong learning. 2. Anticipating learners' needs and adapting the learning environment in accordance with evidence-based best practices. 3. Embracing new skills, knowledge, and standards in the profession as they relate to teaching, learning, technology, and innovation.	**D. Grow**

Preface: The Spirit of Librarianship

For me, Explore epitomizes the spirit of librarianship. My personal under-standing of this started with my own elementary school librarian, Anne Banks Kitchens. Some librarians remember the libraries of their childhood as stereotypical quiet "shushing" places, against which they're determined to rebel—but I don't. Mrs. Kitchens had both a megaphone and a karaoke machine in her school library for daily use! She expected and empowered us to engage thoughtfully with the world and make our voices heard.

In Mrs. Kitchens's school library, there was never any doubt that there was a huge, wide world out there for us to explore, using all the means available to us. The world of technology was smaller in those days, of course. However, Mrs. Kitchens used print materials to bring far-flung parts of the world within our reach. My earliest memory from her classes, as a first grader, is of a nonfiction read-aloud. I don't remember the title of what she read, but I do remember very clearly the way she finished reading and then told us, "And then something *wonderful* happened—the Berlin Wall came down!" In a single stroke, she shared important recent knowledge with us, taught us how to think critically about how information sources may go out of date (the book she was holding was a few years old, from before the wall fell), and modeled a passionate interest in history and geography and how they change the context we live in.

The school library was full of ways to feel immersed in anything we wanted to know and explore. Maps and globes were regular fixtures in Mrs. Kitchens's lessons. So were a variety of hands-on science demonstration tools, including human anatomy models, insect specimens under glass, and a wooden lever device you could hit on one end with a rubber hammer to send a plastic frog flying from the other end. (Obviously, you would then measure how far the frog flew, and collect multiple rounds of data to analyze and interpret.) Once a year she would bring in the Star-Lab, a portable planetarium, and transform the school library into a place where we could crawl directly into outer space. There among the stars, she would share information about astronomy and meteorology with us, as well as stories of the constellations and how the ancient Greeks and Romans understood the cosmos. And of course, in Mrs. Kitchens's school library I could access anything and everything I wanted to read. To top it all off, she had a terrific old ball-and-clawfoot bathtub painted like an American flag that I could snuggle into with my books.

When I was in the fourth grade, my class participated in a schoolwide activity in which we had to select our "True Colors." I identified as Green, which my classmates were ready to let me know was the nerdy color. However, Mrs. Kitchens (also a Green) showed me that it really meant I was eager to know anything and everything, and that the school library was exactly the right place for curious learners like me to thrive. Because of her influence, I will always believe that the support for curiosity and broad personal interests embodied in the Shared Foundation of Explore is one of the most important aspects of a school library and its potential to impact the lives of learners.[1]

Flash Forward

As a high school librarian at the start of my career, Explore was a major part of the ethos of my school library program. I was blessed to work in a school with a truly diverse student population, a faculty that believed in collaboration, a principal and parent stakeholders who were committed to seeing that we had the resources we needed to serve our learners, and a wonderful co-librarian and library secretary as partners. Many of the educators in our building had less than ten years' experience. We had a strong relationship with our local university, which knew we were eager to accept interns, which meant that we had a constant influx of new ideas and innovations. Our student learners came from every ethnic and socioeconomic background, including English language learners from more than fifty countries. That mix of diversity, innovation, and support was the perfect setting to "discover and innovate in a growth mindset developed through experience and reflection" (AASL 2018, 104).

At first, I had an experience that I suspect many new school librarians have. After learning in graduate school about ideal visions for school libraries, I went into that wonderful school, with those wonderful conditions, and was completely mystified when other educators weren't lining up to collaborate with me! What quickly grew our program and services, however, was gradually building relationships with other educators through an Explore lens. We made a regular practice of encouraging curiosity among these educators, and then seeking to provide resources and find solutions to satisfy it. Exploring technology options was particularly helpful; whenever I needed to win over another educator who'd never collaborated with a school librarian before, I introduced a new tech tool or format that we could tinker with together and to see how it might improve their assignments. This gave us a means of consistently embracing new skills and learning for ourselves as well as our colleagues, thus situating the school library as a central professional learning network within our school.

Explore also emerged as a means of handling the bulk of student learners who visited our school library (400+, about a third of our school, every day) and the huge variety of questions they had and problems they needed to solve. At first, I wondered if I needed to be an expert in everything learners might need to know. But soon enough, after it became clear that that would *never* happen, I learned to be extremely comfortable with modeling my own transparent learning to them in response to their questions. "I don't know, let's ask Google!" became something of a catchphrase in our school library. We couldn't possibly teach every learner about all of the technologies they would need to know, so instead we taught them to iteratively "poke buttons and see what happens!" And whenever they found a solution, either by searching it out or by stumbling upon it, we encouraged them to engage with their community of fellow learners by sharing their solutions around the room.

Gradually, we built our school library environment so that exploration was a central value in how both educators and learners interacted with our space. We took pride in becoming the go-to people for all manner of "this might sound crazy, but is there a way to. . . ." questions. We built strong relationships with other educators so that they would feel safe taking instructional risks and trying new things with us. We thought aloud through problems and challenges together with learners, partly to model our thinking processes and approaches to them, and partly because their learning work frequently informed and stretched our own learning. Explore embodied the way I approached layering, deepening, and extending my professional practice as a school librarian.

Learning beyond the Library

After serving as a high school librarian, I had the opportunity to move into school library supervision at the district level. Those who know me well realize that I don't make any bones about how steep my learning curve was during that transition—I had a *lot* to figure out, and all of it in a hurry, while people depended on me to lead! I'll confess that it was a heavy emotional lift, as well as a heavy learning lift; I felt incompetent, frankly, and I wasn't used to that lack of confidence. Fortunately, however, I was able to turn the full weight of my experience as a school librarian onto my own learning curve. I was going through the same kinds of struggles that my learners had felt during challenging assignments and the same kinds of creative risks that my educator partners had felt while collaborating on new ideas and methods with me. So, I did exactly what I had always helped them to do: I worked hard to deliberately adopt "a growth mindset developed through experience and reflection" (AASL 2018, 104) and I dove into exploring my new role.

One of the major lessons I've learned in the last seven years, as a district supervisor and advocate for school libraries, is that the Competencies and Alignments delineated in the *National School Library Standards* Explore Framework represent exactly what stakeholders love about their school libraries. School libraries are centers of learner-directed choices driven by individual interests and curiosity—which is *exactly* what the movement for personalized learning environments is about. By teaching learners to discover, innovate, inquire, persist, and iterate, school librarians are helping learners become truly ready for college, career, and community, with boundless possibilities for their futures. Administrators, parents, and community members all want to see their school libraries function as the heart of the school, where learners' diverse interests intersect and turn learning from something academic into something that changes lives. And when they see a student learner participate in the kinds of school library programming Explore describes, those stakeholders' simple "oh, cool!" reactions can turn them into advocates working to ensure all learners have access to effective school libraries and school librarians.

When districts engage in strategic planning and think "why school libraries?" the Explore standards are exactly what I hope they'll think about. If a school library needs funding for physical renovations and flexible furnishings, I hope the conversation will be around "ensuring that multiple learning activities can occur" and creating "a learning environment conducive to independent and collaborative exploration and problem solving" (AASL 2018, School Library V.B.2–3.). If a school is considering installing a makerspace, I hope their plan includes the school librarian "modeling persistence through self-directed tinkering and making" (AASL 2018, School Librarian V.B.3.). If educators are concerned about how to ensure they're raising student learners who can navigate their online worlds critically and responsibly, I hope these educators plan to partner with school librarians to get learners "reflecting and questioning assumptions and possible misconceptions" (AASL 2018, Learner V.A.2.) and "open-mindedly accepting feedback for positive and constructive growth" (AASL 2018, Learner V.D.3.). And as each district strives for better outcomes for their kids, in their conversations about professional learning as well as student learning, I hope they will focus on "enabling learners by helping them develop inquiry-based processes for personal growth" (AASL 2018, School Librarian V.A.3.). With Explore as the center, all members of the school community have a clear "why" for supporting effective school libraries.

NOTE

1. Readers may enjoy knowing that Anne Kitchens and I are still friends. I returned to her library several times in middle and high school to volunteer, which helped inform my career choice. We connect occasionally on social media, and several years ago I was honored when she attended my wedding!

Introduction: Developing a Compass for Professional Learning

During my very first semester as a school librarian, I had the opportunity to attend my first AASL conference, when the *Standards for the 21st-Century Learner* and *Empowering Learners* were still new. I remember attending session after session on theory and technology and educator collaboration, with presenters who are still among the most popular in our field, taking notes furiously so I could share every detail with my other young school librarian roommates as soon as we all returned to the hotel that night. I left the conference feeling inspired—and daunted! It had been a terrific professional learning experience, but also a profoundly overwhelming one. There was *so* much learning to do, and I wasn't sure what to do with it all. I'd heard several presenters say words to the effect of "don't fret; remember, it took me ten years to get to this point." But I didn't feel like I had ten years—my school community deserved the best *now*.

In my current role as a school library supervisor I see other school librarians go through this same emotional rollercoaster when processing professional learning. Sometimes it happens because they're new and trying to find their footing in a complex field. Other times it affects experienced folks who are trying to climb out of a professional rut while juggling the needs of their families, or feeling frustrated by shifts in their school contexts that bring competing and difficult-to-reconcile pressures on their time and attention. By far, one of the most common concerns I hear from school librarians is how they can deal with having one more thing put on their plate.

This is my intended destination for this book: to the best of my ability, I'd like to help everyone cut down on that overwhelming "one more thing" feeling regarding AASL's *National School Library Standards for Learners, School Librarians, and*

School Libraries, and specifically with the Shared Foundation of Explore. My goal for this book is to support you in aligning Explore with what's already on your plate, rather than piling more on top. Ultimately, I hope to help readers feel like Explore aligns with all the other ideas and trends you're bombarded with daily as an educator so that you can feel better equipped for the kind of high-quality, effective practice you want to provide for your school community *now*.

Approach to the Journey Ahead

Explore is my favorite of the Shared Foundations. I love it because the Competencies and Alignments it covers run the gamut from the most traditional of school library activities—reading widely and deeply—to the least traditional—tinkering and making. I love that this one Shared Foundation brings together the full spectrum of the services school libraries offer, so that instead of being different and disparate things we're supposed to manage, they'll merge into one big theme of helping learners understand all the ways they can explore their interests and the world around them. That wide range of learner competencies, all under the same umbrella, means that Explore can be read as something of a manifesto for much of what happens in our school libraries.

By the same token, my approach to this book has been to think about the vast spectrum of content knowledge school librarians are expected to master and implement—from educational psychology to community economic shifts to bodies of theory from the wider field of librarianship—and to look for ways to make it more coherent and streamlined under the single umbrella of Explore. Rather than an inside-out approach, in which we might discuss the AASL Standards and then connect them out to their broader implications, I've taken an outside-in approach, in which we'll discuss some of the big ideas and trends school librarians are facing and then bring them back in to the Shared Foundation of Explore. My hope is that by doing so, we'll be able to build an understanding of the AASL Standards not as something that all our other tasks must pile on top of, but as a coherent and streamlined framework that informs, undergirds, deepens, and supports all of our tasks.

You'll see quite a bit of narrative in this book; as well, I use personal tone in many places. Why is that? Because you are a person, and so am I. We're humans, and human beings are wired for narrative—it's how we encode our reality. If the intent of this book is to make the lofty AASL Standards feel like they're an achievable reality in the midst of our crazy jobs, then we need to be able to crack their code, and narrative is one of the best tools for doing that. So throughout the book, when new ideas are introduced, you'll see them anchored in stories about other professionals. These stories are intended to provide a starting point for readers who might not have encountered these ideas before, so that they'll have a starting foundation to participate in the learning discussion that follows and to firmly situate the AASL Standards and Explore in real life implementation, right where they belong.

Getting Equipped to Explore

This book is organized according to a simple metaphorical question: what equipment does one need to Explore? I'm sure there are many fine answers to that question (as there always are with a metaphor), but the fundamentals I selected are a Compass, a Backpack, and Boots. When we embark on a long journey, these three things will point us in the right direction, ensure we're carrying everything we need, and support us as we get moving. Even if we're not quite sure exactly what the intended destination might be (in true exploratory fashion), those items will keep us oriented so we don't get lost, allow us to carry the tools we need to use along the way, and protect us when we need to wade through a swamp or climb over a fallen log.

In the Compass section, we'll take a big-picture look at how work is conducted in school libraries, including some of the traditional strengths school librarians lean on as well as some of the contemporary opportunities available for us. These chapters will be organized by the five interconnected roles of the school librarian, as described in the introduction to the *National School Library Standards for Learners, School Librarians, and School Libraries* (AASL 2018, 14–16). Because in-depth professional learning can occasionally seem like it's asking us to throw out everything in our past experience and start over, these chapters will also include some intentional discussion of what Explore does and does not ask us to change in our practice.

In the Backpack section, we'll look at five of the biggest ideas and trends in education right now and how they can have a strong impact on school librarianship. These chapters will be organized to discuss each idea in depth, reel it in and show how it connects back to the Explore Competencies and Alignments, and finally give some examples of what implementation might look like. These examples include short feedback on what might make one type of implementation stronger and more aligned to the AASL Standards than another, in order to help illustrate how to use these ideas to work smarter rather than harder.

In the Boots section, you'll find a detailed Planning Guide to support real-life implementation. Because any set of standards or trends matters only when it shows up in effective services to learners, this section is designed as a self-guided workshop on how to think through the big ideas in this book (or elsewhere), figure out what will get you the most bang for your buck in your school library, and then go through the hard process of making all the myriad decisions required to turn it into action. This section would ideally be completed by a group of several school librarians and/or other educator colleagues who can lean on one another and give each other feedback throughout the process as they learn together.

Professional Wanderlust

The AASL Standards serve as a point on the horizon for all school librarians to aim toward, and Explore offers excellent tools for working toward getting there. However, no two school librarians will take the same path along the way, though many may cross nearby territory or pause at the same landmarks. Every school librarian's journey will be different because they are all traversing different environments of school sizes, demographics, funding levels, staffing levels, principal expectations, parent expectations, and district supports. So when we study the AASL Standards, we must commit to the dual blessing and curse of our professional individualism, which is generally a blessing because we have the autonomy to "discover and innovate," per the Key Commitment of Explore, but sometimes a curse because we can't ever just do what's worked for someone else.

Not only can school librarians not travel the same well-trodden paths as others, they can't even count on ever actually reaching their destination! Professional work is never really complete. Rather, it is iterative, demanding that we exercise a "growth mindset developed through experience and reflection" (AASL 2018, 104) to wake up every morning and try again at something new, gradually refining both our products and our processes along the way.

What is vital in our approach to work, then, is to find joy in the journey itself. We are well equipped with our Compass of services to keep us oriented toward our school communities, plus a Backpack full of resources and ideas to help us grow and thrive along the way. And putting on our Boots with thoughtful, reflective practice will enable us to make the best decisions possible to support the unique needs of our learners. As you work through this book as part of your professional development, you'll have a chance to do your own exploring as you study Explore.

PART I

Compass

Many school librarians entered the field with one of the most fundamental motivations: we all believe the love of reading is critical to a rich and satisfying life, and we all want to promote it to the learners in our care. This isn't because we are quaint bibliophiles overcome with nostalgia for a mythical past in which everything was better; it's because we believe passionately that a better future is possible when individuals' minds are opened, and that reading is the very best universal vehicle for mind-opening. However, many school librarians worry that our job is changing, and that various pressures are gradually choking our ability to do this powerful work.

The perception of how quickly libraries are changing is near-universal, as are school librarians' feelings of being overwhelmed by the process. Many of us feel exceptionally frustrated by the ongoing staffing and budget cuts, fixed rotation schedules, and outdated perceptions that plague our working situations all over the country. With all that going on, school librarians sometimes find themselves in a professional conundrum regarding the AASL Standards. We know we're supposed to implement them, but that can seem unreasonable to add on top of our existing workloads when we're having trouble fulfilling even the basic core work we've striven for in the past.

Explore provides us a Compass to find our way out of this cognitive quagmire. Compasses are essential tools for navigation, pointing us in a consistent direction so that we always understand where we are in relation to it. In this way, the AASL Standards are not just one more thing to add on top of our current workload; rather, they define the basic core of our work and what we can hold steady during periods of turbulence.

The Compass section of this book is designed to illustrate some of the ways the Shared Foundation of Explore defines the school librarian's roles and guide both our traditional strengths and our contemporary opportunities. It puts our work in context with the best of our heritage and the most challenging of our present and future, and offers a sense of direction, so that we can more accurately and coherently assess where we are and where we want to go. Within this context, we will be better equipped to sort through the onslaught of change in our profession and determine which ideas are firm paths forward, which are quicksand, and which are bridges to new territories. Explore ties into the reasons many of us entered the field and gives us a direction to pursue the powerful opportunities ahead.

1
Traditional Strengths

The majority of community members I've met have overwhelmingly fond memories of their youthful experiences in school and public libraries while growing up. Sure, a few remember stereotypical shushing harridans, and some less-than-stellar portrayals in pop culture have furthered those mental images. Still, most people remember their own libraries as magical, happy places where they could find books on anything they liked, get help answering any kind of kooky question they could cook up, and curl up to read. These libraries of memory were lovely oases of calm, tolerance, and egalitarian kindness in the midst of hectic and sometimes not-so-pretty lives. Some even remember the bookmobile's visits as being far more exciting than the ice cream truck's!

We know, of course, that it wasn't magic that made these environments and services so positive; it was the concerted efforts of a strong corps of school and public library professionals. These folks were and are on the front lines of serving their communities, defining democratic information sharing and providing constitutionally protected equal access to marginalized groups. If information is power, then librarians of all types are among the most powerful people on earth, and in our country, they have used that platform to systematically empower others for generations. And as school librarians, we are among the lucky inheritors of a tradition that specifically aims to empower our youngest citizens.

This profoundly powerful work is not a nostalgic artifact of the past, but is our current mission. It is accomplished through the lens of our profession's Common Beliefs (AASL 2018, 11–13):

1. The school library is a unique and essential part of a learning community.
2. Qualified school librarians lead effective school libraries.
3. Learners should be prepared for college, career, and life.

4. Reading is the core of personal and academic competency.
5. Intellectual freedom is every learner's right.
6. Information technologies must be appropriately integrated and equitably available.

These traditional strengths can serve as our Compass, pointing us consistently to what we and those we serve hold most dear: assisting people at their point of need, promoting reading, and engaging the community so that all learners have opportunities to think, create, share, and grow. When we are clear about our core, it is possible to stretch and mold our everyday execution of these ideals to meet the needs of a shifting environment without losing focus on what's most important. Let's look at how these core services appear in Explore through the school librarians' roles of program administrator and information specialist, as defined in the AASL Standards (figure 1.1).

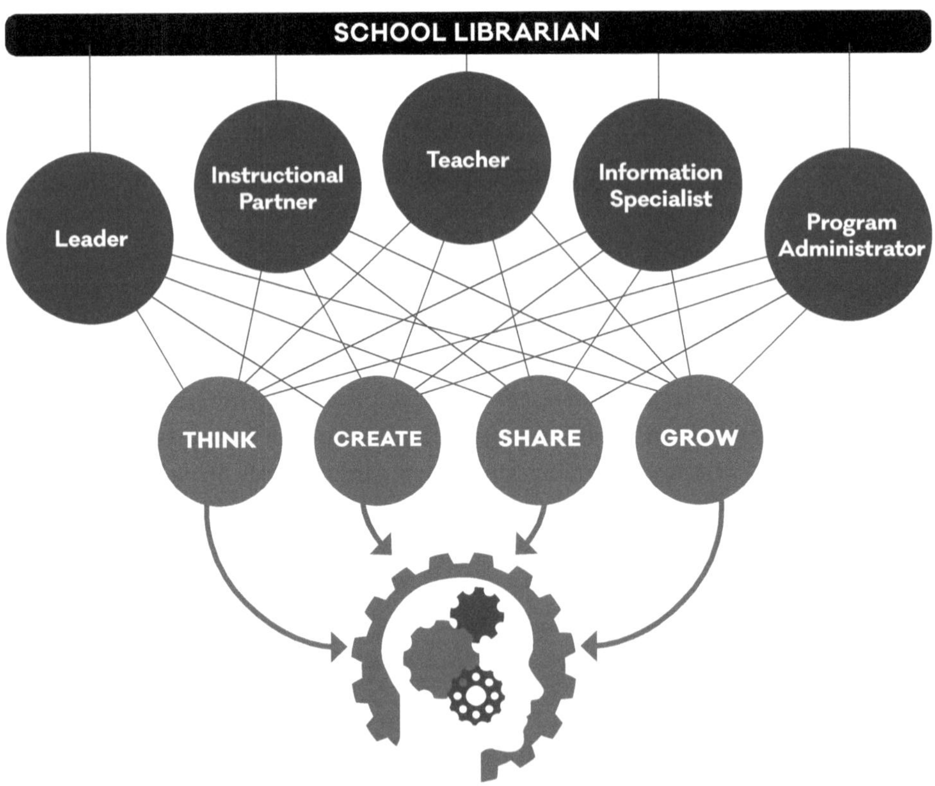

FIGURE 1.1 / **Learners experience school librarians' roles through Domains**

Explore in the Role of Program Administrator

The school librarian's role of program administrator includes some of the least conspicuous but most fundamental parts of their work: managing people, budget, and space to ensure equitable access to resources for all learners. In everyday implementation, this can include lofty things like strategic planning and seeking outside partnerships, but it can also include workaday tasks like recruiting volunteers, running book fairs, and putting up bulletin boards that will make learners feel welcome. This is the work that underpins grand visions and turns them into action.

Many aspects of this role do not change when implementing the AASL Standards. For instance, Explore calls for us to "[encourage] families and other members of the community to participate in school library activities" (AASL 2018, School Library V.C.2.). This is a strong echo of the community-oriented library experience that so many of our friends and neighbors remember and hold dear from their childhoods. This Alignment reinforces what effective school librarians know, which is that the wider the audience we work to serve, the richer the experiences we can provide for learners. As program administrators, bringing in families and community members allows us to connect with volunteers who can significantly augment the way we're able to staff our spaces and services, forge relationships with donors who can make financial contributions to fund the diverse resources our learners and school communities need, and continually assess constituents' perceptions of our physical and virtual spaces so that we can align and strengthen our services.

As another example, Explore asks us to "[ensure] that multiple learning activities can occur in both physical and virtual spaces" (AASL 2018, School Library V.B.2.). Part of our role as program administrators has always been to structure and schedule our spaces so that we can serve our learners and school community at point of need. That includes time set aside in our work for instructing whole classes, helping individual learners and educators with whatever needs come up spontaneously, and everything in between. Further, it includes creating visual cues within our facilities by using furniture or signage or other media to make clear that all of these activities are welcomed and valued in our school libraries, and that they can occur simultaneously in their various zones without competing with one another. These aspects of structuring our time and spaces may not be noticed by our school communities, but they are part of our deliberate work to create equitable access for everyone we serve.

While Explore does not ask us to change these aspects of our work, it gives us room to incorporate modern shifts to streamline practice and respond to constraints and opportunities. For instance, while responding to multiple types of learning needs is best done on a fully flexible schedule with a co-librarian and at least one clerk, not all school librarians have those options within their school structures. However, we have many tools that can help get us closer to the ideal. Modern automation software can enable self-checkout stations that learners can be trained to use, so circulation is available when the school librarian is busy working with a full class. Online learning management systems give us the ability to create instructional modules that can be inserted directly into our learners' classes so that we can maximize the audiences we are able to reach. And where bringing in community experts to speak to classes once required major logistical efforts and expenses, now it can be done with a simple online video meeting. These functions have, to a degree, been used in our practice, but today's technology makes them so easy to access that it would be a tremendous missed opportunity not to exercise them fully.

Explore in the Role of Information Specialist

The role of information specialist is one of many school librarians' favorites. This is the role that includes hunting down resources to meet niche needs, piloting virtual gadgets and gizmos to dream up exciting ways to use them in learning, and triumphantly connecting educators and learners to the exact answers they're looking for, especially when library users were worried that the answers might not exist. This is the role that makes librarians famous for knowing everything—or, if not, for being able to find it!

Implementing the AASL Standards plays very well to this traditional strength. Explore emphasized this in its very first Competency, asking school librarians to encourage learners to "[read] widely and deeply in multiple formats and write and create for a variety of purposes" (AASL 2018, Learner and School Librarian V.A.1.). If that isn't an internal Compass pointing to what school librarians hold most dear, I don't know what is! Promoting a love of reading—encouraging the vaunted magical moment that arrives when a learner is matched to their just-exactly-right book—is what gets many school librarians out of bed in the morning. Many educators work with their learners to promote reading well and passionately, especially at the elementary level, but it's their role as information specialists that sets school librarians apart from the others. As information specialists, school librarians are unmatched in knowing the literature; being aware of a tremendous breadth of authors, series, and genres; and engaging in readers' advisory to figure how to convert a learner from reluctant reader to passionate bibliophile. School librarians do this not only at the individual level but also at the group level, collaborating with other educators to curate sets of high-interest, high-quality resources. And when they couple that with another Explore Competency, "fostering opportunities for learners to demonstrate personal curiosity and creation of knowledge through engaging with a wide variety of resources and technology" (AASL 2018, School Library V.A.2.), this type of collaborative effort can turn classroom studies from merely adequate to rigorous and engaging.

While this Shared Foundation does not ask school librarians to give up any existing work that promotes reading and high-quality resources, the Explore Competencies and Alignments do invite us to consider an ever-broader spectrum of what reading and resources might include. The "and technology" and "in multiple formats" phrases of the Explore Competencies and Alignments have exciting implications for how we can expand and enrich this most cherished part of our work. Explore calls for reading of any format we can imagine—magazines, graphic novels, e-books, audiobooks, zines, blogs, recipes, social media threads, cereal boxes, Dad's baseball cards, auto repair manuals—to be considered a valid and valuable part of readers' journeys. Explore invites us to specialize in information resources that may not even be text-based; photographs, primary sources, vinyl records, cartoons, paintings, artifacts from Grandmother's attic, and travel souvenirs are all formats that can enrich learners' experiences. And by considering technology as part of the wealth of resources we collect, Explore encourages us to assemble both low- and high-tech production methods, from die-cut machines to movie editing software, that will enable our learners to produce new information as naturally as they consume it.

Everything Old is New Again

Frequently, the perception of perennial change cycles in schools and insatiable learning curves for professional educators has to do with the proverbial pendulum. It swings back and forth every few years, with changes in leadership bringing philosophies that move from one extreme to the other, then eventually returning to ground that has already been covered (and likely proven ineffective). Almost every experienced educator probably has at least one story to tell a newbie that starts with "Ah, yes, you've had a lovely 'brand new' idea, but we tried that a few years ago when..." This perception can leave us feeling cynical and reluctant to expend energy on seemingly ephemeral initiatives.

Holding firm in our foundations in the field, and using those as a Compass to navigate our way through new pressures and expectations for our work, is what will help us reduce the feelings of being overwhelmed that can undermine our ability to grow strong practices. Please note that this is not encouraging us to continue doing what we have always done! Instead, it is a call to continue focusing on *why* we have always done it. When we can build strong patterns between the new and the old that incorporate effective, modern ways of practicing into our time-tested priorities for serving learners and communities, the mental clutter that surrounds us will be reduced, allowing us to see a bright and clear path forward.

COMPASS CHECK

Questions for the Reflective Practitioner

1. What elements of your practice are you most proud of, and where can you find them echoed in Explore?
2. How might your school library benefit if you are able to draw connections between Explore and the current expectations, initiatives, or shifts being communicated to you from your building and district administrations?
3. What might be some ways you can lean on your traditional strengths as a program administrator and information specialist to contribute to innovation in your building and district?

2

Contemporary Opportunities

When the COVID-19 global pandemic first became widespread in the United States in early 2020, everyone—and that meant *everyone*—felt its impact. Some communities were hit harder than others by the disease itself, but no sector of the country was left untouched by the economic fallout. In schools, that fallout led to widespread closures, anguish about the traumatic home situations many learners and their families had fallen into, miserable budget decisions in which there could be no winners, desperate scrambles to create more equitable technology access, urgent learning curves for educators to become proficient at online instruction, and existential arguments about the roles schools should or should not be expected to play in reopening the economy.

The magnitude of this interruption to our social fabric meant that everyone—again, *everyone*—must reexamine their priorities for the long run, regardless of whether the virus personally impacted them. When schools began reopening, many families (in my district, about 30 percent) made the difficult choice to switch from the classroom to virtual learning in order to keep their children safe. Many other families made the equally difficult choice to send their children to socially distanced classrooms that bear little relation to their previous experiences, in a desperate attempt to balance their physical, mental, and economic health. With no good choices available, everyone had to do the best they could to live according to their most important values.

For school libraries, living out our values includes holding the AASL Standards steady while considering timely shifts in our delivery mechanisms to better meet the needs of blended and virtual environments. Our job has not fundamentally changed, but the tools and strategies we use to accomplish it have. If we manage this shift effectively, we may find that our profession has not only weathered the storm, but emerged better than before, with a strong new skill set and an eager corps of collaborators. All of us in education are recentering on our core priorities for serving learners, which has the potential to point us all toward a future that we can not only accept, but aspire toward.

Possibilities abound for school libraries as learners and educators explore this "new normal." Our traditional Common Beliefs (see chapter 1) still hold firm, but they have exciting implications for implementation through methods that existed previously but are gaining special prominence in modern conditions: virtual and blended learning, around-the-clock resource access, and serving adults as learners. These contemporary opportunities can serve as our Compass, pointing toward the horizon of what can become achievable with new expectations, needs, and technologies at our disposal. Let's look at how these possibilities appear in Explore through school librarians' roles of teacher, instructional partner, and leader, as defined in the AASL Standards.

Explore in the Role of Teacher

The school librarian's role of teacher is one of the easiest for most outsiders to the field to understand. It includes duties related to—drumroll please—teaching! Although almost everyone can visualize the whole-class instruction we often deliver, we also teach in more varied and flexible ways. We often work one-on-one with individual learners at point of need, or with small groups of learners divvied up while collaborating with a classroom educator. We can be the lead educator responsible for a whole class at times, or we can team teach equally with another educator, or we can act as a learning support for a class while another educator takes the lead. When our school structures allow us to work on a flexible schedule, the possibilities for how we teach collaboratively are limited only by our imaginations.

Explore offers us routes to give full rein to that collaborative imagination and ponder opportunities for transformation of our teaching. For instance, it calls for "implementing technology as a tool or resource for learning" (AASL 2018, School Library V.B.1.)—an Alignment that seemed innocuous prior to the COVID-19 pandemic, but now looks like the lid to Pandora's box. There was a time when we might have thought that meant we should teach a class how to use social bookmarking to organize some web resources and then called it a day.

But now—now! After experiencing a mighty shift in prospects and possibilities, the whole field of education has a different outlook on the appropriate expectations for technology in learning. Now we know we might need to teach full class groups, or even whole courses, online. We know that our instruction can be synchronous, with a wide array of tools for real-time interaction with learners who tune in from any location, or it can be asynchronous, to truly support our learners on a 24/7 basis. Freeing our teaching work from the strictures of geography means we can easily "beam in" expert visitors from around the country to be part of our lessons;

it means we can share strengths with other librarians we know, trading lessons between buildings and expanding our learners' support networks; it means we can easily instruct whole grade levels at once, freeing up scheduling options for our collaborating educators; it means we can embed our instruction modules directly into our collaborators' courses, as if we were present in all of their classrooms simultaneously, without ever leaving the school library unattended. And those are only a few practical considerations for our own teaching workflows, never mind the options available for learners to choose and own and transform their knowledge products!

What Explore does not change, even during colossal interruptions like those brought by the COVID-19 pandemic, is our fundamental responsibility to serve our learners in our role as teacher. Even if we find ourselves in a fully virtual school environment, cut off from accessing our own school library facilities and print collections, we are responsible for finding instructional routes to ensure that we are preparing our learners with the knowledge and skill sets they'll need. Our educator partners—classroom teachers, administrators, school counselors, and everyone else in K–12 education—are facing similar struggles right now. What will happen if some of us are not yet experts in online instruction and don't feel ready to help learners as they need and deserve? Well, we'll learn, that's what. All of us will learn alongside our student learners, and show them what growth-oriented, resilient lifelong learners look like.

Explore in the Role of Instructional Partner

The school librarian's role of instructional partner is related to, but separate from, the role of teacher. The work of our role is the collaboration that happens before and alongside instruction, including all of the planning and design work that makes teaching successful. In the ideal situation of a flexible schedule supported by clerical staff or a co-librarian, the role of instructional partner entails engaging in in-depth collaboration at the point of need, resulting in co-taught classes and units, perhaps even leaving the school library and going into the classroom if needed. If we're not in that ideal situation, the role simply looks different: we snatch a few minutes of collaborative conversations with busy educators while walking down the hall, or we work asynchronously on shared online planning documents, or we devise schedules that will allow school library rotation classes to match and complement classroom needs.

In a world in which all educators must fundamentally rethink their routines and methods, Explore gives us productive anchor points to help our collaborative partners reenvision everyone's work. For instance, we are charged with "establishing and maintaining a learning environment conducive to independent and collaborative exploration and problem solving" (AASL 2018, School Library V.B.3.). In a less connected past, we might have interpreted that Alignment to refer to arranging our own school library facilities with a mixture of individual reading nooks and large conference tables, so that learners could engage in different types of tasks in our physical environment. But as we prepare for a dynamic future, we can think more deeply about environment as a cognitive condition for learning, and how designing instruction around student ownership and personalization theories can improve our learners' exploration and problem-solving experiences.

The current seismic shifts in the educational landscape give us an unprecedented foothold as instructional partners to influence other educators' thinking around Explore's discovery and innovation competencies in their digital classrooms. Many of our collaborators will feel like first- year teachers again, and they'll need and want all the help they can get; so, as we adjust to our own learning curves in this environment, this will be a beautiful opportunity to support them as adult learners.

However, as always, we need to remember that our collaborating educators (like all people with information needs) *can't* know what they *don't* know, and therefore may not be able to ask us very good questions. This has always been a limitation of human cognition, and our need for change cannot change this; in fact, extreme stress conditions may make it worse. To be effective instructional partners, it is our job to envision a future of digital exploration and then proactively seek out educators and learners who will benefit from what we bring to the table.

Explore in the Role of Leader

For a school librarian, the role of leader is more important now than ever. This role includes keeping an eye on the challenges and opportunities facing school librarianship and education, developing ideas and solutions to support the members of our school communities, and building and maintaining strong relationships with stakeholders. Leadership does not demand that we be "in charge," but it does demand that we use our personal influence to help those around us move in a positive direction.

The Shared Foundation of Explore offers some clarity on how school librarians can lead and influence their school communities using Competencies and Alignments that will be exceptionally important during and following a major digital transition. For instance, Explore asks that we commit to "leading other educators and learners to embrace a growth mindset through lifelong learning" (AASL 2018, School Library V.D.1.). This simple phrase, which before the COVID-19 pandemic might have sounded like a few warm and fuzzy buzzwords, now demonstrates that we can make powerful contributions to the resilience and strength of our communities. It calls us to lean into relationships and help those around us understand that it is okay to be vulnerable because we're all on a steep learning curve, that all small steps are worth celebrating when they're headed in the right direction, and that we are here to walk this road alongside them.

If there were ever a time in history for "embracing new skills, knowledge, and standards in the profession as they relate to teaching, learning, technology, and innovation" (AASL 2018, School Library V.D.3.), this is it. Luminaries in our field have long called for anytime/anywhere 24/7 access to the high-quality resources and learning experiences that school libraries provide; we now have the opportunity for this access to move from pipe dream to common reality. As leaders, we know these ideas are not just for school librarians, but for all educators who care deeply about ensuring that their work positively impacts learners' experience and, through them, the world.

Although it might feel like we've been asked to lead the whole world through a ring of fire, remember that our profession is exceptionally well equipped for this work because we have always done it. We were made for responding to needs, researching solutions, and leading the way in harnessing resources to make a better world for others, and our AASL Standards reflect that. A time of exceptional need simply makes that work especially timely and visible.

Answering the Call

Our traditional strengths called us to hold steady to our foundations in the field and use those as a Compass to navigate our way through new pressures and expectations for our work. Our contemporary opportunities call us to use that Compass to point ourselves firmly toward the horizon. There has never been a more important time to make sure that our personal fears, discomforts, experiences, and learning curves do not limit the potential of what we may become.

In many parts of the country, school librarians fear that their work will not be valued as a funding priority in this new environment. There is precedent for this fear, from past waves of budget cuts in the 1990s when school internet access became increasingly available, and then again during the Great Recession. Today's conditions combine the worst of both of those, accelerated to a breathtaking speed. Some districts have already made moves to cut school library positions as an emergency means of balancing their budgets, and in others, school librarians feel like they're waiting for the proverbial other shoe to drop.

As we know, effective school libraries will be more important than ever in a world where learning not only uses virtual platforms for knowledge building and information sharing, but depends on them as lifelines. But it is up to us to spread the good word about the value we bring to this environment, and to back up our words with high-quality services every single day. The best way to advocate is not to wait for bad news and then storm the castle, but to proactively claim a place at the table while entire school communities are reinventing themselves.

COMPASS CHECK

Questions for the Reflective Practitioner

1. What current needs in your school community are most pressing, and where can you find them echoed in Explore?
2. How might your school library benefit if you are able to firmly connect your building or district's reinvention efforts to your own biggest dreams for your practice?
3. What might be some ways you can use contemporary opportunities as a teacher, instructional partner, and leader to contribute to the efforts of your building and district as they move forward?

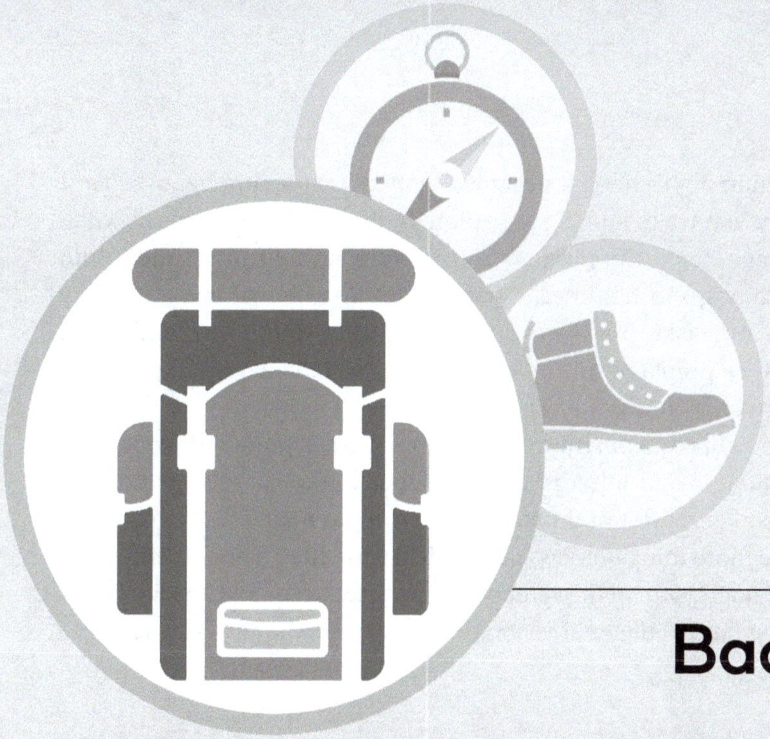

PART II

Backpack

Abraham Maslow, famous for his hierarchy of needs, is also credited with the famous assertion "I suppose it is tempting, if the only tool you have is a hammer, to treat everything as if it were a nail." This is a simple but powerful illustration for a human tendency that frequently gets in our way: our brains have a strong bias for the familiar. This is not the same as being reluctant to change. Rather, it means that even when we sincerely want to change or try something new, it can be hard to make progress in a new direction. This happens because we see everything through the lens of our prior experience and methods, which may not be a good fit for the new task at hand. When we try to envision a new practice—to use Maslow's tool analogy, let's say we want to learn to cut tile into smaller pieces for a kitchen backsplash—if we see it with only our old tools in hand, all we'll find is problems. One can certainly use a hammer to make a tile into smaller pieces, but it's not going to produce that backsplash we wanted!

As school librarians, we may be ready and willing to embrace the Shared Foundation of Explore in our practice, but still have trouble visualizing it. Similarly, we may have other great ideas flying at us from every direction—from the wider field of librarianship, from other roles in the field of education, from the everyday needs we see among our learners—that we want to respond to but can't figure out how to fold into our everyday duties in the school library. It all feels like one more thing on our plate, and as mere humans, we can only do so much! Our existing repertoire of professional knowledge is behaving like that metaphorical hammer in these cases. As effective as that repertoire may be for the things we're currently doing, it needs to expand before we can accomplish new tasks.

The Backpack section of this book is designed to increase the number of tools at our disposal so that when we're looking at Explore in the AASL Standards or when those great ideas come down the pike, we're not stuck trying to beat them into former practices with only our hammer in hand. Nothing will ever beat the trusty hammer for hammering tasks. But if we also have a drill, a band saw, and a belt sander in hand, we'll be prepared to stop thinking of our main job as hammering, and start thinking of it as building.

Similarly, with the right content knowledge in hand, we can gradually stop thinking of the AASL Standards and other important education ideas as something to add on top of our main job, and start thinking of them *as* our main job. At that point, instead of being "one more thing on the plate" to deal with, they'll be something we won't have time and energy *not* to implement. Explore plus a full Backpack of tools will powerfully prepare us to enact our vision of a better future for our learners.

3

Learning Commons

In the spring of 2016, a school library in my district faced a crisis. Its learner and educator usage had dropped off dramatically since the school implemented 1:1 laptops several years earlier, its third school librarian in three years had resigned, and it was saddled with a facility that had had no functional upgrades (other than the now-obsolete desktop computers) since the 1960s. And just before classes let out for the summer, an environmental scan found that the school library's ceiling was full of asbestos. Executive Principal Tim Berry could have taken the easy way out: get through the basic asbestos abatement but otherwise not put up a fuss, and let the school library trickle its way toward oblivion. Instead, he made a commitment that he would not put it back the way it had been, no matter what steps were necessary. Instead, he was going to build a school library that would improve his whole school community.

Because he was between school librarians that summer, Mr. Berry started work with a team of stakeholders including his administrative team, master teachers, PTSO leaders, and school board representative. Together they envisioned the school library as a true hub of their school, a center for personalized learning, technology innovation, and thoughtful participatory behavior that would weave through all of the school's academic and cultural initiatives. Ever since their school's 1:1 laptop rollout, they had expressed frustration with the feeling that they had "a twenty-first century school stuck in a nineteenth century building," and they wanted to see their school library as a flagship space rich with cutting-edge information use and technology to pull them out of that perception. They said they wanted a school library that would "feel like Starbucks," abuzz with self-directed work and purposeful conversations. They wanted all furniture to be flexible and mobile so that they'd be able to totally make and remake the space inside ten minutes. And they wanted traditional tasks (like learning research skills and accessing information) to move out of the school library and into the classroom, taking advantage of their 1:1 technology, so that more avant-garde tasks (like project-based learning, STEM makerspace, and robotics and engineering) could move into the library as the school's center of innovation.

I had the pleasure and honor of supporting Tim and his team as they successfully partnered with our district's maintenance team and a generous alumnus of the school, resulting in a school library renovation worth about half a million dollars. The result is a truly beautiful space, but that is not what makes it worthwhile and exciting. The value of the new space is that, under the leadership of an effective school librarian, the library will be collaborative, participatory, responsive, and innovative—a true learning commons, ready to support its learners in exploring their way to college, career, and community.

In Your Backpack: Learning Commons

The learning commons is not a tool, nor a program, nor a thing you "do." Nor is it another example of the proverbial pendulum swinging back and forth in education, putting new words on the same old ideas. Instead, the learning commons is a way of reframing school libraries—why they exist, what they look like, what role they play in the school—to emphasize and ensure their relevance in the modern school context. Anyone who has ever thought "good grief, it's all changing so fast!" about the expectations of their school library will be familiar with the impetus for the learning commons, which at its roots is about responding to change. The term emerged from some soul-searching conversations within the profession, after internet access and Google searches started to become ubiquitous and schools began questioning whether they still needed school librarians. In *The New Learning Commons: Where Learners Win! Reinventing School Libraries and Computer Labs* (2008), David Loertscher, Carol Koechlin, and Sandi Zwaan began defining and exploring this fundamental professional shift in philosophy and function.

In many ways the core functions of school libraries haven't actually changed much at all over time. A glance at the Common Beliefs defined in the *National School Library Standards* (AASL 2018, 11–14) points to reading, intellectual freedom, and equitable access, which have been major undercurrents in librarianship for many decades, as long as school library standards have existed. And a quick review of Ranganathan's *Five Laws of Library Science* (1931) boils down the most important guiding precepts of our work in a way that still looks remarkably fresh:

1. Books are for use.
2. Every reader his book.
3. Every book its reader.
4. Save the time of the user.
5. The library is a growing organism.

What has changed recently is the context in which those core concepts are carried out. It cannot be denied that technology is important to learners. It pervades every aspect of their lives. Online resources and digital tools are critically important parts of our collections, as much or more so than print in some cases. Digital access means that the function of the school library facility is profoundly different because users do not have to go to a single physical location for information access. It also means the school librarian's job is executed with very different emphasis, because while every user already has easy access to "something," they may not understand how to make good decisions about what they're accessing, or what they will do with it. So while we retain Ranganathan's traditional precepts to organize resources in a way that facilitates access, matches resources to needs, and continually develops the school library, we must execute those duties in a way that includes digital citizenship, multimedia production, and anytime/anywhere virtual services, while responding rapidly to new needs as they emerge.

"The library is a growing organism," then, becomes one of our most important guiding principles for guiding learners' explorations—and is the root of the learning commons. It is less a new thing to do, and more a new way of doing business to assure and assert that our school libraries grow and change in response to the growing and changing needs of our users, and thus ensuring our continued relevance in schools. In an update to their earlier books, Loertscher and Koechlin (2014) defined four characteristics of a successful learning commons, useful for organizing our discussion.

CHARACTERISTIC 1: A collaborative physical and virtual environment that invites and ignites participatory learning.

In a learning commons, the most important thing to consider in establishing the school library's environment is that it is user-centered. If one were to take an audit of some of the most basic trappings of a traditional school library, however, we'd find things like these:

- Large circulation desks that commandeer the library's entryway
- Heavy wooden tables with floor marks to make sure they stay in the right place
- Newspapers on poles and magazines in plastic covers to prevent them from being stolen
- Security gates and "tattle tapes" to prevent books from being taken
- Tight limits on how many books can be checked out and how often they can be renewed
- Fines for late returns of items
- Cabinets in back rooms for storing office supplies
- Lengthy annual orientation lessons to explain all of the school library's rules

Notice that many of those things are aimed at preventing the user from doing something wrong. And if the starting presumption is that the user will probably do something wrong unless prevented, then the environment is centered around protecting the "stuff" and ensuring the school librarian's control.

When we shift to an environment that is centered around the user's needs, we see a lot of those control measures broken down. Large circulation fortresses are replaced with smaller, nimbler desks that communicate approachability. Supplies are placed out front where users can help themselves. Self-checkout allows learners to manage their own materials (and, as a bonus, frees up the school librarian's time to do more important things). Magazines and newspapers are placed conveniently near comfortable seating so they can be casually flipped through. Furniture is lighter, on wheels whenever possible, and is moved around in different configurations based on what kinds of activities educators and learners want or need, especially for collaborative work in various types of groups. Signage and space flow should make it easy for learners to intuit how to do the right thing on their own so that instructional time can emphasize how the school library and its resources are designed to empower learners. All of these shifts communicate trust in users so that they will feel welcome to be in the space and make it part of their lives.

Our digital spaces, too, are an important part of the user-centered school library environment. Rather than treating the school library's online presence as something extra, it should be seen as the virtual door to the library, where learners can enter our space and use our services 24/7, whenever they need them. Digital versions of our in-person services should be created and extended whenever possible. For example, if we have a physical display to promote our new books, then we should have reviews of those new books linked on our websites and promoted on our social media accounts. Breaking down physical/digital barriers is an inclusive approach, as it allows us to serve our communities regardless of individual challenges with scheduling, transportation, or physical or social needs that may affect in-person access. When our virtual presence is an equally important part of our environment, we suddenly have the ability to extend the school library far beyond its facility's four walls and the hours it is open because it can be embedded in classrooms and homes and anywhere else it is needed, at any time.

CHARACTERISTIC 2: **A responsive dynamic that is invested in schoolwide improvement through an evidence-based process of design, modify, rethink, redesign, and rework.**

If we decide what changes to our school libraries will make them learner-centered without actually consulting any learners, then we really have not achieved our goal of inviting and igniting participatory learning! That's where the idea of a responsive dynamic comes in. Throwing money at facility renovations and new websites creates only a veneer of updates, not a true learning commons, unless we have truly embraced a philosophy of putting learners at the center of our practice and responding to their needs. We can do a lot of work at the latter without spending a dime, by asking our communities for input, early and often, and making shifts accordingly, on an ongoing basis.

In traditional modes of service, school librarians are justifiably proud of our abilities to serve users by answering questions. But how often are we the ones doing the asking? This is an essential part of the work of the learning commons. It can take a wide variety of forms, from annually surveying our whole school communities about their needs, to touching base with other educators about whether the materials we've pulled were adequate to serve their learners in a given lesson, to perking our ears up when our principals and districts discuss their priorities and thinking "how can the library be part of that?," to just plain watching for learners' most commonly asked questions and treating them as serious feedback about what we need to build and serve. Sometimes, if we're honest, we haven't asked our users many questions about their needs and desires because we're afraid of what we might hear; it might be too far a departure from our current skill sets, or from the time and effort we're willing to put in, or from the funding and infrastructure and support we have available to make changes happen. It is up to us to model the lifelong learning we want for learners and show a little vulnerability by asking questions about their hopes and dreams, even if those aspirations aren't yet connected to the school library, so that we can effectively respond and design our services for those who need them.

Just as "books are for use," our facilities and services exist for use. That means they must be designed for those who need to use them. This is why it's so important that furniture should be flexible and change day by day or even hour by hour. Our space needs to serve the activities taking place, not the other way around! If the learning that happens in our school libraries is defined and limited by its physical surroundings instead of by learners' needs, then we have dramatically missed the boat. It is the same for our print and digital collections, in that they should be able to quickly respond to new information about what learners need. As soon as we hear that the content standards of educators in other disciplines are changing or that they're offering a new class, we should be updating our consideration files with new resources that we can purchase to support them. Our digital resources can be especially responsive because we can update our online offerings to share helpful links, documents, apps, and the like within a few minutes of identifying the need.

CHARACTERISTIC 3: Professionals who can successfully lead out front, or lead from the middle, or push from behind are great candidates to head a learning commons.

Alongside these shifts in environment and modes of service, the school librarian's role has to shift. Any school librarian looking at this chapter and thinking "I can't do all of that on top of my current work" is probably right. No one can do everything.

We can, however, shift what we do. The learning commons model calls on us to accomplish that shift partly through trusting and empowering our users through our participatory environment so that we can give up many tasks related to control, and partly through leadership, so that we can enlist more hands in carrying the load.

The learning commons model calls on us to join forces with other people and departments so that the school library's reach is expanded by sharing the load. In schools, we all have essentially the same goal: to send our learners out into the world ready to thrive. The different parts of our organizations have different specialties, of course, but when we focus on what we have in common, tremendous opportunities for partnership emerge. School librarians can and should show ownership over the national shifts in science and social studies standards, both of which include language that has tremendous overlap with our own AASL Standards. We should also assert ourselves in technology initiatives, to some degree in terms of hardware and to a greater degree in terms of instructional technology integration. As all parts of the school start to orient toward increasing multiple literacies, opportunities to partner around effective text use and research and media production are no longer limited to English language arts, and extend to the arts, world languages, and career and technical education. When school libraries make a point of being part of the solution, working alongside many partners working toward the same goals, we are able to dramatically increase our relevance and responsiveness to a wide variety of services to learners.

At the same time, joining forces does not mean duplicating efforts. School librarians have a different job title and licensure than other educators for a reason. We have a different expertise and a different lens to bring to all of these common goals! When our time is limited, school librarians get the most bang for our buck when we spend our time doing those things only we can do, using our specialties of resource connection and instruction to serve many partnerships. The beauty of partnership is that we do not have to be in control of the whole process of everything that happens in our school libraries. When we contribute our best work and we trust our partners to contribute their best work, wonderful things will happen for our learners as a result of pooling our time and talents.

As leaders in the learning commons, we cannot wait passively for these partnerships to come to us. There is an excellent chance that all of those science and social studies and technology and arts and career-tech partners don't know what we can bring to their work, or we would be partnering already! So it is up to us to reach out and form those connections, and to continue following up and nurturing those connections for the long term. Consistent care and feeding of partnerships is harder work, frankly, than just managing our own spaces. However, the payoff for taking on that challenging work is much greater than the sum of its parts. When school librarians invest our time in leadership, it will pay dividends for our learners by bringing cohesion, participatory learning, and responsive dynamics to their experiences throughout the school community.

CHARACTERISTIC 4: Participatory learning through attention to excellent instructional design, using best resources and technologies, and building personal expertise and collaborative knowledge are the work of the learning commons.

None of the shifts we've so far discussed will matter until they result in student learning. The everyday work of the learning commons is not to buy new shelves on wheels, nor to update our school library websites with more links, nor to orchestrate impressive-looking stakeholder meetings. All of those things must be done in service of the school library's most important outcome, which is to nurture student learning.

Learning commons proponents have a saying: instruction must be just in time, not just in case. In designing our school library services, that means the idea of being responsive and dynamic extends to our instructional planning. Examples of "just in time" instruction might include many of the lessons you already teach: using an online database to find sources for a research project, evaluating point of view and authority in sources related to content studied in the classroom, creating a multimedia project to showcase what's been learned over the course of a unit, and so forth. The trick, however, is that these lessons are taught right when learners need them. "Just in case" instruction, on the other hand, is delivered whenever it's convenient, in the hope that it might prove useful at some point in the future. That might include any of the same lessons, if the access/evaluation/media skills are taught in isolation instead of in connection with what learners need to know for their classroom learning. It may also include many time-honored lessons like orientations or "library skills" rotations, which are usually delivered with the goal of better preparing learners for success in all kinds of projects. But remember, if our services are designed to prevent problems from happening, then we're starting from an assumption that our users will cause or have problems, so we probably need to fix something in our environment to make sure we can use more positive assumptions. If instruction is not centered around the users' immediate needs, then it is unlikely to be practiced or remembered, and that means the time was wasted. If instruction comes right when it is needed, however, it will make a significant contribution to our learners' experiences.

As school librarians, our own skill sets must also be responsive and dynamic. Whatever is coming down the pike—new school reform initiatives, emerging technologies, changes in the publishing industry, challenging political environments that affect our communities—it is our job to learn about it, to figure out how our school libraries need to respond to it, and to invent solutions if they don't yet exist. This responsibility means we will always face some level of ongoing uncertainty about our work, and that is okay. When we try something, perhaps get it wrong or have an incomplete understanding, and then engage in an ongoing process of seeking feedback, modifying, and wholly redesigning our work when necessary, we're modeling exactly the kind of iterative lifelong learning that we want our learners to adopt to face the uncertainty of their own lives. Building and maintaining our personal/professional learning networks (PLNs) is not an option or a nicety; it is a critical part of our work. If we allow ourselves to become isolated or work in silos, we will not be able to introduce the ideas and make the connections that our learners need from our school libraries.

Learning Commons in Explore

In the Shared Foundation of Explore, the ideas behind reframing the school library as a learning commons are closely matched to several of the AASL Standards. Although Explore is not the only Shared Foundation in which some parts of the AASL Standards reflect a learning commons philosophy, this concept is clearly embedded within Explore. A closer look at Explore will reveal some of the direct connections between this Backpack item and our standards.

ANTICIPATING NEEDS AND ADAPTING

If we were to describe the learning commons in a nutshell and situate this body of theory within the Shared Foundation of Explore, it would certainly be accurate to say that it calls for "anticipating learners' needs and adapting the learning environment in accordance with evidence-based best practices" (AASL 2018, School Library V.D.2.). Explore asks us to consistently adapt the learning environment, which includes both our physical and our virtual spaces and programming, to serve our learners' needs as they grow, change, and shift direction. It specifically asks us to make these changes in accordance with evidence-based best practices, which means that we are not tasked with blindly asking our users what they want and then fulfilling their requests. Rather, we are to use our expertise to match their feedback with our content knowledge about multiple literacies, the wider field of education, and the changing information landscape in the world outside our schools, and then to blend those sources of input into a consistently responsive and continuously improving service model.

Sometimes our learners won't realize that they need something different. It's our job as professionals to anticipate their needs and respond by watching for trends and patterns outside the school library and redesigning our services accordingly. School improvement plans and educational reform movements are a prime place to look for those trends and patterns, as are consumer technology shifts and college and career prospects. Responding to these wide-ranging needs may prompt us to actually redefine what constitutes "library stuff." School counseling, ACT questions, translation services for English language learners, PTSO volunteer coordination, education services for parents, outreach by local museums or symphonies—if they are designed to respond to our learners' changing needs, all these and more belong in the school library environment.

The expectation that school librarians must anticipate needs can feel like we are suddenly supposed to become mind readers—but in reality, this is a pretty basic principle of librarianship that has been around as long as libraries. The humble reference interview, which most of us learned in our preservice programs, addresses the basic truth that most people don't quite know what they're looking for when they start a search. Librarians are trained to ask follow-up questions and "listen between the lines" to help their users clarify their thinking to form a more targeted query before starting an information search targeted at what they really need. Readers' advisory works the same way; each time we guide a learner through figuring out what kind of books they might like and then make recommendations accordingly, we have mediated their thinking, anticipated their needs, and custom-adapted our responses. The learning commons model asks us to go beyond traditional reference inquiries and serve our users in all parts of the school library experience, in both our interactions with the school community as a whole as well as with individuals.

SERVING MULTIPLE GROUPS' NEEDS

One of the factors in a learning commons that some school librarians find complicated is that it can be difficult to constantly respond to all needs when each of our learners and each segment of our school community will have different needs at different times. Sometimes those needs may even seem to compete with each other. And there are only so many places we can be and changes we can make at one time!

With a little planning, however, Explore does not actually require us to clone ourselves. (Whew!) Rather, what we need to do is consider the underlying "bones" of our school libraries, our program infrastructure, and "[ensure] that multiple learning activities can occur in both physical and virtual spaces" (AASL 2018, School Library V.B.2.). In this way, we create space ahead of time for multiple and differing needs to emerge organically. In the physical space, this could mean setting aside different corners of the school library for individual and group work, arranging furniture so that there are clearly separate whole-class and walk-in spaces, or training other educators and student helpers to handle circulation and other technical tasks in one part of the school library so that you can leave your desk and work on instructional facilitation in another area. In the virtual space, this could mean promoting peer-to-peer readers' advisory through social media and participatory features of the online public access catalog (OPAC) so that learners can get book recommendations even when they're off campus, ensuring that all educators know how to use your online database subscriptions so that they can access high-quality resources on the spot in their classrooms or other computer labs, or publishing screencasts and exemplars online for the school library's frequently asked questions (e.g., citation formats, school-wide technology platforms, common hardware troubleshooting) so that users can access help even if they can't directly access the school librarian.

Because we cannot in fact be everywhere at once, if we do not build this infrastructure for serving multiple, simultaneous needs we will actually meet very few needs other than our own need for feelings of certainty and control. This is not an acceptable trade-off. But for those who fear the weight of shouldering this infrastructure burden, remember that you are not in this alone; this is the reason that "commons" is in learning commons, and why it emphasizes leadership. It is also why we must start with the presumption that we'll trust our users. We have to give away control and empower others in order to make all of that complex and simultaneous support happen. If we hold responsive dynamics as our constant vision, we really don't have to face such an overwhelming rate of change all the time. Instead, there will be different daily details, but they will always be attached to the same focus on meeting user needs.

ESTABLISHING THE LEARNING ENVIRONMENT

In the learning commons, individual or small-group activities are just as important as whole-class activities, and they require a similar commitment from the school librarian to consider the school library's infrastructure and plan ahead to meet a variety of different needs that may occur simultaneously. All parts of the school library, big and small, can impact its ability to meet these diverse needs. It is essential to consider both the big picture and the tiny details as part of school library administration, because "establishing and maintaining a learning environment conducive to independent and collaborative exploration and problem solving" (AASL 2018, School Library V.B.3.) is crucial to developing lifelong learning among the many members of our school community.

For individual learners (as opposed to those visiting the school library in a whole class), their first need is often to feel intellectually safe. It can be a real risk to walk into a new space and ask a question, especially when it feels like it's about something everybody else seems to know already. Plus, if we're honest, a big, busy school library with tons of activities and choices can be intimidating for someone who doesn't know their way around! This is where something as humble as signage can make an enormous difference for our learners. Clear, direct, simple, and ample signage lets our users know how to navigate the environment and do the right things on the first try. Brochures and handouts, coupled with a friendly and navigable web interface, can give learners a way to answer their most commonly asked questions with a sense of safety. When it helps them intuitively self-manage, those pieces of the environment mitigate learners' sense of risk, so that they are comfortable venturing a more substantial intellectual risk in their creative or inquiry work. And of course, our most important tool for mitigating risk is a friendly face and a nonjudgmental response to needs.

Collaborative groups may have a need for intellectual mess and noise. Public schools are often not very good places to be messy. As much as the field has talked about dismantling the "factory model" of education in recent decades, we are still saddled with funding and staffing structures that make it necessary to move large groups of learners through times and tasks efficiently, and that means keeping them pretty tightly locked into a narrow set of possibilities for what they should be thinking or doing at any given time. The kinds of creative thinking and multiple literacies we know they need to develop for thriving in the modern world, however, demand divergent thoughts and behaviors, especially when it comes to collaborating with peers. Educators share this increasing need for divergence. In the learning commons model, the school library can function as a haven for this by providing easy ways to manage the intellectual mess. Tables that can be easily moved into groups, small group rooms or moveable screens that can block out noise, storage space for projects in process, whiteboards, and online tools for facilitating and recording collaborative means of communication—all of these school library services contribute to an environment in which divergent thinking is allowed and valued.

The Shared Foundation of Explore emphasizes the importance of the environment as it supports exploration and problem solving. If the school library environment is a reflection of the ideas, values, and needs of its users, then the shifts we make in our physical and digital spaces must embody the values of participatory learning and collaborative problem solving. To show and maintain these values within the environment itself is a highly inclusive approach, a way of working to ensure that we meet any and all of the diverse needs that come through the door. Individual, small group, and whole group needs are all important, and they shouldn't have to compete. Users should be empowered to create the conditions for all of these activities on their own, through self-management and configurable space.

SERVICE PARTNERSHIPS AS ADVOCACY

Advocacy is not a stand-alone activity. In fact, the "alone" part is inherently counterproductive. Explore defines effective advocacy for school libraries as "building and advocating for strong relationships with stakeholders who recognize and support an effective school library" (AASL 2018, School Library V.C.3.), with emphasis on strong relationships throughout our school communities. It will always be something we do together with our partners, not something it's advisable or even possible for us to try to do on our own. Perhaps one of the most important aspects of the learning commons model is that relationship-building is inherent in its everyday work. Each and every time we modify some part of our services to better respond to our users' needs, we are extending the hand of partnership and helping them recognize and support an effective school library.

Of course, we should also support that everyday relationship-building work by issuing clear and regular communication about it. Not every member of our school community will be physically present or in direct virtual contact with us at all times, and we wouldn't want them to be, even if it were possible, because if they are utterly dependent on us, then we probably have not accomplished our job of empowering them to connect with resources independently. Regular publicity should come alongside our services. Like all other parts of the learning commons, this is most effectively done if all communications keep the user at their center. Communications should be about what our stakeholders need and want to know (how a new online resource will help parents help their kids with homework, how to locate hi-lo books for struggling readers in the school library catalog, how a learner's independent inquiry was deepened by using the school library to connect with resources), not only about numbers that are convenient for us to count and report (circulation statistics, gate counts, number of books weeded). We have to consider the most convenient ways for our audience to receive information. Some segments of our populations will be best reached via social media, others via our websites, others through our learning management systems, others with a good old-fashioned paper newsletter; if that means we must publish the same content in multiple ways to ensure the word gets out to everybody, then it is absolutely worth the effort!

In education, we often talk about the proverbial swinging pendulum. Every time it swings, the field is trying to solve a problem: literacy rates, inclusiveness, career preparation, and so forth. What if the solution could always be found in the school library as learning commons, no matter the direction of that swing? Bringing together a vast array of services, activities, resources, and the ability to anticipate future needs, all under one physical and virtual "roof," is perhaps the best thing we can do to ensure our value to stakeholders. This model gives us the chance to be part of the solution they're looking for, regardless of which way the shift is heading, and it gives us the flexibility to shift right along with it. Our stakeholders want what is best for learners. When we embrace the learning commons philosophy in our school libraries, we have the chance to build strong relationships and enlist advocates by showing that we want the same thing.

Learning Commons: Implementation Examples and Analysis

Everyday implementation of the principles of the learning commons and the Explore Alignments to which they're tightly connected can take a wide variety of forms in the school library. Following are several implementation examples, with each pair contrasting more- and less-effective executions of a similar idea, in the context of Explore's four Domains. The accompanying analysis notes are designed to help you understand what makes one example of practice stronger than another, so you'll be able to reflect on how their elements compare to your own practice and make decisions about some areas for professional growth you might like to pursue.

DOMAIN: THINK

Scenario: You want to improve learners' confidence in using online databases.

Example A	Example B
• Teach learners, educators, parents, and administrators to think of their school library website as the virtual door to the library, where they can access the virtual side of any resources or services they would see physically in the school library facility. • This includes online databases and web resources, interactive chat and backchannel through social media, and collaborative documents for soliciting input on the collection and upcoming events.	• Post a variety of online databases and web resources, grouped by subject area, for learners to access via your school library website. • Work with classroom educators to schedule orientation lessons to show learners how to use them in their assignments.

Both of the examples make high-quality online resources easily available to learners. Only Example A, however, uses the virtual learning commons to invite participatory culture and collaboration, with quick ways of updating based on feedback. Example B treats resource access as static one-way communication, with the school librarian rather than the learner at its center.

DOMAIN: CREATE

Scenario: You want to ensure that multiple types of activities can take place in the school library.

Example A	Example B
• Use furniture to create different zones in the school library: computer lab near the door, story rug in front of the wall-mounted video presentation screen, tables behind the rug, independent study carrels on one wall, soft seating near the circulation desk.	• Collect furniture that allows for different zones in the school library: small flip tables that can be linked in different sizes and shapes, comfortable bucket seating that can be stacked out of the way when needed, video presentation screens on mobile carts. • Arrange furniture the way it will work best for each group or lesson; coach learners in how to move it around to meet their needs.

Although both of the examples create a physical space that allows for multiple activity types, Example A is static and restricts activities to those allowed by the way the space is configured. Example B is likely a bit messier, but it is dynamic and allows for making the space meet user needs, rather than the other way around.

DOMAIN: SHARE

Scenario: You need to advocate with stakeholders for funding, in order to achieve positive outcomes in the school library.

Example A	Example B
• At the beginning of each year, attach a copy of the AASL *Definition of an Effective School Library* to a list of funding requests and send it to the principal and the Parent-Teacher-Student Organization. • At the PTSO meeting, bring a slideshow with lots of images of books and learners reading and using the computers. • Ask other educators to tell the principal why the school library is important. • Sign up to speak at the school board meetings on the importance of school library funding.	• Request an annual beginning-of-year meeting with the principal to discuss the school's goals for the year and the AASL *Definition of an Effective School Library.* Brainstorm what the school library is currently doing that's well aligned with both, what it can start doing that would better serve the school's goals, and what it can shift away from in order to free up resources for the new work. • Take those ideas to educator partners and learners for feedback on the best way to implement the shifts. • Present the school library's shifts to the PTSO to answer questions and collect more feedback. • When everyone is bought in to the vision for the school library, seek funding to make it a reality.

Both of these examples demonstrate significant effort from the school librarian to advocate for the library and its funding needs. However, in Example A the school librarian is focused on driving the message and pushing it to multiple audiences, while in Example B, the school librarian is focused on building relationships and creating a feedback loop to ensure that everyone shares and is working toward the same goals. Example B may take longer to achieve results, but is likely to have better results in the long term by enlisting more partners in the effort.

DOMAIN: GROW

Scenario: The principal tells you she's interested in creating a makerspace for the school.

Example A	Example B
• You volunteer to take the lead on making it happen. • Browse some books and journal articles in addition to social media, and notice that there are many different ways to collect materials. • Bring together a group of learners, educators, and parents to think about what kinds of maker activities would really match the needs of your school, and then research what kinds of materials will make those activities possible. • Request donations and some PTSO funding to buy those materials. • Work with stakeholders to decide that the best place to locate the makerspace is in an empty classroom on the sixth grade hallway, where you and the other educators can collaborate on supervising learners in it, depending on needs.	• You agree to make it happen in the school library. • Look at a few ideas on Pinterest, and notice that it seems like anything goes, and all kinds of materials are okay. • Put the word out to other educators, parents, friends, and community members that this is a terrific way to clean out their closets and donate all their unused craft supplies. • Request some PTSO funding to raid the craft section of a local store, and look for a grant to buy a 3-D printer. • Quickly amass a wide variety of supplies learners can use, and clean out an office space to store everything. • Allow learners access to the space to make anything they want whenever they have free time.

Although both of these examples entail hard work, creative thinking, and enthusiasm on the part of the school librarian, Example A does a significantly better job of anticipating learners' needs and adapting the environment accordingly, especially with stakeholder input. Example B starts with the "stuff," rather than starting with learners' needs, and it is driven solely by the school librarian throughout.

COMPASS CHECK

Questions for the Reflective Practitioner

1. Think about the everyday tasks you do to keep your school library running. Which ones do you tend to do out of habit or because "that's what school libraries do," and which ones do you do in a response to an identified need within your school community?

2. When you make a change in your environment, collection, or services based on feedback you've received, how do your users respond? What does it mean to them to see that you've heard their voices?

3. How can you create feedback loops to ensure your school library is constantly growing in response to needs? What are your annual, monthly, and daily sources of information about your users?

4. What are the most important things going on in your school, district, or community? Who can you join forces with to introduce those movements into your school library services?

4

Inquiry-Based Learning

"What are your kids bad at?" This is my usual opening line in any collaborative conversation, because it focuses attention toward problem solving. And that's where my English educator team and I started one spring when, due to a nasty coincidence of snow days and new testing procedures, we suddenly found our usual research project plans squeezed out of the calendar. It was going to affect the entire junior class, and we were at a loss for what to do next.

Our traditional schedule would involve walking learners through the entire sequence of topic selection, note-taking, thesis development, outlining, and writing in their English language arts classes, then bringing them to the school library for about a week to dig deep into print and online sources and gather information. To get all fifteen class sections through that process would take about three weeks, and we didn't have that kind of time. Between the snow cancellations and the mandated shutdown of the school library lab for computerized testing, we had about two days left on the calendar to work with. Plus, as we talked around it, my educator partners kept remembering that they hadn't covered logical fallacies yet and would need to do so before the testing started.

So we returned to our planning question: "What are our kids bad at?" After talking through the inquiry cycle, we decided the answer was synthesizing information from multiple sources. Learners had been through the entire traditional research process for multiple years by then, and they had completed all of the associated activities as required, but they still hadn't shown much growth or depth in their ability to analyze and synthesize. Based on this, we decided to go in a different direction.

Our team developed a controlled-source research project. Curating the sources ahead of time and providing copies solved the problem of access to the library and computer lab—plus, we knew that finding sources wasn't what our kids were bad at—so there was no need to allocate limited instructional time to practicing that skill. Learners' deliverable was to be a "fake news" article incorporating logical fallacies, which solved the problem of covering that content before testing season. The time saved by learners' searching for their own sources was used to lean in on synthesis instruction. Learners practiced analyzing details from several outlandish images, constructing a narrative out of those seemingly unrelated sources, and then expanding that narrative by incorporating details from other unrelated articles, ultimately forming their fake news article. They also wrote a reflective process paper, to promote metacognition about their analysis and synthesis and ensure that their total writing length and rigor was appropriate for their grade level.

From a traditional vantage point, some might say that we didn't have learners do any "real" research. After all, we didn't let them explore any sources outside the sets we'd curated, and the product didn't actually include any real facts—and admittedly, this is not what we would have done in ideal conditions. But as instructional designers, we knew that searching for facts was not what our learners needed help with. Thinking through the inquiry cycle, rather than thinking through traditional research tasks or activities, helped us pinpoint what our learners really needed to gain from this experience and to find a way to accomplish it within our constraints. This method of instructional planning can open a variety of new routes for learners to learn to explore their world through inquiry.

In Your Backpack: Inquiry-Based Learning

Inquiry-based learning is the kind of term that makes a school librarian's heart fill with joy—finally, an educational movement that is tailor-made to get us involved that makes us essential to the core of the school's work, so we don't have to try to break in from the edges! For many other educators, however, it is the kind of phrase that can inspire pretty mixed reactions. Some will find it tremendously exciting, the embodiment of their goals for learners and the reasons they wanted to work in education in the first place. Others will receive it as a euphemism for chaos, a stream of idealistic buzzwords that can never work in the real world. The truth is probably somewhere in between.

Inquiry-based learning presents enormous opportunities for learners to situate what they're learning in authentic contexts; to relate their learning to real-world problems that they're concerned, curious, or passionate about; and to exercise feelings of ownership over their own learning by making choices about what they'll pursue and how they'll express their findings. This is how adults learn, and it is a beautiful thing when we can build that natural process into our learners' school experiences. However, not all inquiry learning is created equal, and we won't fulfill its promise if the process isn't taught well. Many educators are asked to implement inquiry-based learning without actually understanding what it is and how it works, and it's difficult to imagine that scenario resulting in tremendous success. Fortunately, we have a variety of well-established frameworks and methods to draw on that will help us understand how to implement inquiry learning successfully.

There are quite a few inquiry frameworks out there, and different people choose among them for different reasons, especially when it comes to aligning with local forces such as school or district initiatives. It is perhaps easiest to define inquiry-based learning by looking at a few of the most well-known frameworks.

- Guided Inquiry Design was developed from an extensive base of research about inquiry learning by Carol Kuhlthau, Leslie Maniotes, and Ann Caspari (2012), including Kuhlthau's influential Information Search Process and incorporating perspectives from K–12 curriculum design and museum education. It is ideally meant to be implemented as a way of teaching within a fully personalized learning environment, not just a structure for isolated research projects. Its steps are Open, Immerse, Explore, Identify, Gather, Create, Share, and Evaluate.
- Big6 was created by Mike Eisenberg and Bob Berkowitz (1990), a pair of educators who have held multiple roles, including experience as school librarians. It is popular and widely used, and its language is closely matched to what is traditionally used in many English language arts curricula. Its steps are Task Definition, Information Seeking Strategies, Location and Access, Use of Information, Synthesis, and Evaluation. There is a spinoff called Super 3, from the same authors, which is aimed at primary learners and uses just three steps: Plan, Do, and Review.
- The Stripling Model of Inquiry, developed by former ALA president Barbara Stripling (2003), grew out of her collaboration with Judy Pitts on the research process and was later refined toward inquiry through her research and practice as a school library supervisor and educator. It has been featured as a resource in the Library of Congress's Teaching with Primary Sources program that is aimed at supporting social studies educators. Its steps are Connect, Wonder, Investigate, Construct, Express, and Reflect.
- Design thinking is a methodology associated strongly with science, technology, engineering, and math (STEM) but applicable to cross-curricular problems and pursuits. The concept comes from researchers as far back as the 1950s, but as a framework it is most famously associated with the Hasso Plattner Institute of Design (2010) at Stanford's d.school, that defines its steps as Empathize, Define, Ideate, Prototype, and Test.

The ins and outs and distinctions of these inquiry models, as well as the wide variety of others out there in the world of pedagogy, are beyond the scope of this book. This discussion is centered on the Shared Foundation of Explore, after all, rather than on Inquire! However, it is important to understand the broad commonalities between frameworks that make up inquiry learning, in order to see how it connects meaningfully to the other items in our Backpack.

FEATURES OF INQUIRY LEARNING

Every inquiry framework, regardless of its origins or what content area it tends to align with or what vocabulary it chooses, starts with some variation on exploration. Inquiry learning does not come out of a vacuum. Instead, it naturally starts with something the learner is familiar with and then, upon identifying a gap of some sort, proceeds into something the learner is curious about. The expression of curiosity might vary in different situations. In literary research, that expression might look like defining a thesis statement regarding a character's intentions; in an engineering task, that expression might look like capturing an idea for an improved product or process; in a historical investigation, that expression might look like challenging an accepted interpretation of events. The connection between what we know and what we don't know, the opening of a little chasm in our knowledge, gives us a deep urge to fill it. The rest of the inquiry process is merely a way of systematically responding to that fundamental urge.

Though the frameworks are systematic, another feature they all have in common is that they are meant to be iterative and recursive. Inquiry is an inherently messy process! It is natural and predictable that when a learner is acquiring knowledge at one stage of an inquiry process, some part of that knowledge may send them back to an earlier stage to refine their thinking and try again. In the Stripling framework, for instance, a learner may have been knee-deep in their Investigate phase, searching and analyzing sources, when they encounter a piece of information that is so interesting or powerful that it sends them back to Connect and Wonder about something new; or that learner may make it all the way to Express, when, in the midst of refining their thoughts into something they can present to others, they realize there are gaps in their information that they must return to Investigate further. At times, this recursion can be so profound that the next iteration goes in an entirely different direction than the earlier work—and that is totally fine, because the new direction is almost certainly more effective and more interesting for the learner!

A third commonality between inquiry models is the necessity of reflection and self-evaluation. Throughout the inquiry process—not only at the end, though that is essential—learners should be taking stock of their work, looking for gaps or inconsistencies, refining their thinking and polishing their products, and noticing how their understanding has changed as a result of their efforts. This continual reflection and evaluation is what contributes to the recursive and iterative nature of inquiry; it's how learners know that they need to go back and make a change or refinement.

When teaching learners to pursue independent inquiry, it is crucial that school librarians and other educators allow for this exploration, iteration, recursion, and reflection. These elements comprise the essence of what differentiates inquiry learning from more traditional modes of classroom learning; they are what make it possible for learners to truly grow their interests and passions, rather than just reproducing facts and getting through assignments. Implementing this type of messy work in a whole-group learning environment requires careful planning by the school librarian and collaborating educators, with plenty of time built in for learners to fully round out the issues they're exploring, work through a few iterations as needed, and reflect deeply. This work calls for deep learning, not quick learning—but when done right, it is ultimately more efficient because learners will retain and carry more of their newfound knowledge forward with them into their lives.

COMMON PITFALLS IN IMPLEMENTING INQUIRY

Inquiry learning does not always fulfill the tremendous potential it promises. The world is full of schools and districts that have bought lavish technology in the name of wide-open inquiry and other optimistic goals, only to lament the devices as horrible distractions that lead to poor learning and poorer behavior. When this happens, it is not the fault of the technology; rather, it is the natural outcome if educators have received inadequate professional learning in how to successfully implement their tools to achieve those lofty goals. When looking specifically at inquiry learning, that usually means a failure to adopt, understand, and fully use an inquiry framework like those mentioned.

Most school librarians will have heard other educators say (or will have said themselves) something along the lines of "I'm just going to have my kids go online and do some quick research today." The assignment that typically comes with this common refrain is some kind of worksheet that requires learners to search online, or sometimes use a preselected website, to look up the answers to a set of questions. Unsurprisingly, learners completing these assignments do not undergo a profound experience of inquiry-based deep learning that broadens their horizons and equips and motivates them to pursue their passions—rather, they typically get through it as quickly as possible and then move on! That is because this type of assignment is not, in fact, research. It might require searching, but that is not the same as researching. It is materially no different from locating facts in a static textbook.

When asked, most learners know that their "research" assignments skip most of the steps of inquiry detailed in common frameworks. Even when asked to conduct a much longer and seemingly more in-depth assignment (e.g., a persuasive essay with pro/con sources or a literary research paper), learners are often required to put in a lot more work at a few parts of inquiry and told to skip the rest. Essentially, many learners have come to understand inquiry as having only two components: search and produce. They feed a query (often a shallow one) into a web search engine, and they feed the results (which they may not even understand) into a paper, presentation, or other product. No connections are made to their personal interests and curiosities, no grappling or deep understanding of the content occurs, and no marvelous character traits like perseverance or motivation for independent learning develop. This is not, contrary to the all-too-common belief, because all the learners are lazy and distracted by excessive screen time! It is because faulty instructional design lacking an appropriate inquiry framework has left out the parts of the research process that ought to produce those desirable outcomes.

For instance, in the simplest of the inquiry frameworks mentioned, Super 3 for primary grades, there are only three steps: Plan, Do, and Review. And yet, most "research" assignments only ask learners to Do, with no attention paid or time allocated for Plan or Review. In assignments that are supposed to use the Stripling model, learners are typically asked only to Investigate and Express; Construct and Reflect are squeezed out of the timeline, and the question of "what did my teacher tell me to do?" ends up substituting for Connect and Wonder. Guided Inquiry can be similarly misapplied when learners are only asked to Gather and Share, with the remaining phases truncated. Design challenges often start with a brief and rushed time allotted to Ideate or even jump straight to building a Prototype. The result can't possibly Test productively if no time was given to the Empathize and Define stages because then there is no way to tell what need is or isn't being met.

Why is poor inquiry design so common? Educators do this unintentionally, but systematically. The steps that do get included in instruction are the visible ones—the ones that get skipped are likely to be invisible. Not coincidentally, the visible steps are the ones that are easier to quantify and grade: an educator can easily tell if a learner has produced the required three source citations, or filled up the required ten notecards, or written the required five paragraphs. Phases of inquiry that feel like activities get scheduled, but phases that feel like internal cognition are assumed. It is not a safe assumption that these internal phases will or should "just happen," if we do not schedule and instruct and assess them! Sometimes, educators may have a gut instinct that they need to guide their learners more intentionally with the internal or invisible phases, but without an inquiry framework to lean on, they simply don't know how. Those phases are where much of inquiry's inherent messiness turns up, and due to the natural pressures and strictures of working in K–12 education, many educators' time and attention are just too overwhelmed to deal with that mess. There is no way to shut down the inherent mess of the inquiry process, except to bowdlerize it until it is something else entirely. Diluted and distorted "research" activities are the result.

However, poor-quality research is not a foregone conclusion. With careful planning and thoughtful implementation of a strong inquiry model that includes all phases, educators have a chance to create truly meaningful experiences for their learners. The primary way to avoid potential pitfalls is simple: educators must allot sufficient time for the messy question definition, planning, and construction of ideas that inquiry demands between and around its searching and production tasks. If there is not enough class time to include those things, then a different instructional decision should be made! It's okay if the entire process doesn't happen every single time—perhaps learners will occasionally be allowed to create a simple annotated bibliography instead of a polished presentation, in order to concentrate their limited class time on refining their questions and searching for available sources; or perhaps educators can preselect the source material for certain projects, in order to focus learners' time and attention on making meaning from texts related to the questions they have generated—and it is preferable to do some of the process well, focusing on different parts each time, than to repeatedly do only poor, shallow work. A culture of inquiry will develop when expert educators (a) build strong relationships in which they can trust their learners with some autonomy over their messy progress, (b) have strong enough content knowledge that they can plan inquiry as an important use of learning time rather than something "extra," and (c) are themselves strong enough inquirers that they can confidently give up control over certain details of their learners' work while still corralling it back to an effective end.

Inquiry-Based Learning in Explore

The Shared Foundation of Explore includes a number of close intersections between the AASL Standards and the principles of inquiry-based learning. However, inquiry is embedded throughout the work of the school library, and as such, Explore is not the only Shared Foundation in which inquiry learning appears. It is worth a careful study of the complete AASL Standards Frameworks to fully understand how the thoughtful and systematic implementation of an inquiry framework can impact a wide variety of aspects of a school librarian's practice; however, that is outside the scope of this book! So for now, we will take a closer look at inquiry within the Explore Competencies and Alignments.

INQUIRY FOR PERSONAL GROWTH

Many school librarians' favorite part of their job is the responsibility to teach inquiry because it is not only about helping our learners through their school assignments, but also through "engaging in inquiry-based processes for personal growth" (AASL 2018, Learner and School Librarian V.A.3.). Unlike some educators who feel locked into a prescribed educational program, we get to nurture learners in pursuing anything and everything they're interested in! When we help our learners master the inquiry process, we're equipping them with the tools they need for independent pursuits, as well as anything they might need in the classroom.

This is not to discount the importance of teaching inquiry within the classroom; it has too much potential for deepening students' learning to not take advantage of it in the course of academic instruction. And besides, the formal use of an inquiry framework is often most easily taught in a whole-class setting, so that learners can see each other working through the same steps, understand the systematic nature of following a framework, and collaboratively identify common stumbling blocks and strategies for getting through cognitive messes. However, pairing academic inquiry instruction with support for learners' personal inquiries is a beautiful way to help them see the connections between their classwork and their lives outside of school. This is how lifelong learners are made.

The learners in our school libraries will have a huge variety of different personal interests and inquiry paths. Maybe they want to know more about their mother's cancer treatments. Maybe they want to know how to become a Dallas Cowboys Cheerleader. Maybe they want to know everything there is to know about how dinosaurs turned into birds, or how horses are trained for the Kentucky Derby, or about the classic cars their parent likes. As school librarians, we are called upon to be information omnivores who are familiar with popular culture, different career fields, and breaking news as well as with the school's curriculum, so that we can help guide our learners through the various stages of the inquiry process no matter what the topic.

It is important in our practice that school librarians very explicitly connect the inquiry process, including all of its stages and strategies, from academic to personal needs. Because inquiry is messy and often challenging, learners may be reluctant to dig deeply into it during their free time, if they don't have a clear understanding of the process they're going through. For instance, if they don't clearly understand that it's natural for the Explore stage (in Guided Inquiry Design) to feel frustrating and confusing before clarity emerges, they may give up and move to an easier way of spending their free time, thus missing out on something that could have been personally meaningful. And if their parents have not independently intuited appropriate inquiry strategies, learners may not have a guide to help them at home. It would be a tremendous missed opportunity to teach all of the stages of inquiry thoroughly in an academic context, but then blindly assume the skills will be transferred to personal lives without further direct support, thus leaving success at home to chance.

LEARNING THROUGH CRITICAL REFLECTION

An excellent way school librarians and other educators can judge the difference between high-quality inquiry learning and low-quality "research" worksheets and assignments is whether they support learners in "reflecting and questioning assumptions and possible misconceptions" (AASL 2018, Learner and School Librarian V.A.2.). When high-quality research with ample time for cognitive mess and recursive work is being taught, learners who are digging into sources that they are authentically interested in and challenged by will naturally start to reflect on what they're finding and how it connects to or perhaps challenges their previous ideas. This reflection may emerge at various stages of the inquiry process, as delineated in the various inquiry frameworks, particularly in the early connecting, exploring, and questioning stages, which are a natural fit because questioning assumptions and challenging misconceptions by incorporating new information is exactly how learners form stimulating and interesting thesis statements.

On the other hand, when low-quality "research" is being assigned, there isn't enough cognitive room (or perhaps even physical room, in the case of worksheets) for these processes. Tasks that require learners only to run simple searches and then regurgitate the results into a product do not allow for these types of complex thinking. School librarians and other educators who are concerned that they do not see this type of thinking in their learners' inquiry work should first step back and examine instructional plans to see if they have thoughtfully and rigorously implemented all stages of the inquiry model they're using. If they are designed well, some of the desired learner outcomes should emerge.

Too many learners who receive inadequately designed inquiry instruction end up trying to do their research backwards. They will arrive at the library for help with a request that sounds something like "I know what I'm trying to say; I just need to find a source that says it." This is the very opposite of questioning their assumptions—instead, it systematically reinforces them! But many plans and assignments invite this type of poor work by focusing instruction and assessment on only the quantity of sources and products. This is just a longform way of demonstrating confirmation bias, and it is no wonder that it does not result in transformed learning experiences.

In well-designed inquiry instruction, however, learners should never have the chance to "know what I'm trying to say" until they have been exposed to a variety of sources in the early connection and exploration stages of the inquiry frameworks. True inquiry should start by introducing learners to new ideas—after all, if they've already processed what they think about a topic, the point of the assignment is unclear—or to a new angle on something they thought they understood. It should invite a new perspective, and allow learners a chance to change their inner worlds by seeking and recombining and reflecting on new information. This is not just a utopian vision of the classroom; it is how real practicing scientists and researchers work, and our learners deserve to access the building blocks of these experiences early, instead of struggling through poorly designed tasks first.

INQUIRY AS INNOVATION

Some educators may fear that choosing and rigorously implementing an inquiry model will limit learners' choices and options for how to pursue their lines of inquiry. However, the opposite is true. Inquiry models do not dictate the activity steps of inquiry; rather, they encode and clarify the processes that naturally occur in our minds so that we can become consciously aware of what is (or should be) already happening when we inquire. We can then harness the full power and potential of each stage. Staying true to an inquiry model allows us to tie our instructional design to cognitive needs instead of traditional activity steps. This opens the door for "co-constructing innovative means of investigation" (AASL 2018, Learner and School Librarian V.C.2.), in which educators work with learners on entirely new means of investigating possible answers to questions, without ties to old or obsolete structures. Topic selection, potential information sources, product and presentation technologies, mastery of selected content knowledge, implications for authentic audiences—all of the forms these elements typically take can be rethought and reconstructed in the context of a well-implemented inquiry model, often with the learners as participants in the construction process.

For example, time-worn tradition dictates that learners begin their research in print reference materials. For some topics, this is an excellent strategy. Reference materials are often the best way to get a concise overview of a complex topic that's been debated for years, to understand the whole arc of the topic before digging into other sources that will illustrate its complexities and debates. And working in print can provide excellent means for learners to immediately adjust and refine their topic as they spot related keywords nearby in the cumulative index or as they browse the shelves to find their sources and notice additional interesting sources that may expand or focus or redirect their thinking. However, other topics may depend on cutting-edge research, or on current events that are unfolding on the news hour by hour, or on phenomena that must be directly observed from an experiment—none of which can be achieved through any reference materials, let alone in print resources. And those types of limitations will be true even in the most well-funded and up-to-date collection; further limitations can stack up rather quickly in school libraries whose budgets make it difficult to sustain print reference collections. Insisting that print reference is where research must start is an outmoded instructional paradigm—but then, insisting that any particular type of source is where research must start will be equally ineffective, and will always result in needless frustration for learners. By contrast, if we teach learners to use the early exploration steps of their inquiry model to expose themselves to a variety of sources and make good decisions about which types will be the most appropriate to gather—which will sometimes be print and sometimes not—then we give our learners agency in co-constructing an inquiry path that will be uniquely suited to their personalized needs and interests.

When school librarians are effectively assisting learners to co-construct innovative means of investigation, grounded in a process defined by a solid inquiry framework, it's okay if they don't use traditional sources. For some projects and interests, the best resource we can choose might be social media; for others, the best method would be to interview witnesses; for others, perhaps we even need to capture authentic writing samples such as graffiti from public spaces. The important parts of inquiry learning are not about sticking slavishly to traditional activities and formats. Rather, the important thing is to find the best way to pursue new knowledge. There is a whole wide world of information available for our learners, and they deserve to use all of it to enrich their inner lives.

STRATEGIC USE OF FRAMEWORKS

It can't be restated often enough: when "providing resources and strategies for inquiry-based processes" (AASL 2018, School Library V.A.1.), the very first strategy that should be employed is to select, instruct, and implement an inquiry framework with fidelity. The vast majority of school libraries are already well-prepared to provide a broad variety of resources to support inquiry through their print and digital collections and makerspaces, but far fewer have well-entrenched inquiry framework habits established among their users.

Which framework should be selected? As with an exercise plan, the best inquiry framework is the one that will be used regularly! Some frameworks may be more easily implemented in certain content areas, by dint of what resources are widely available; for instance, the Library of Congress's Teaching with Primary Sources (TPS) program has the Stripling model built into its professional development resources, so a school librarian hoping to collaborate heavily with social studies educators who have been trained in TPS methods may prefer to start with Stripling. Some frameworks may have especially powerful training or support publications available; for instance, Guided Inquiry Design is famous for its robust summer institutes, professional books, webinars and online resources, and in-person consultation options, all of which can significantly contribute to a school librarian's and collaborating educators' feelings of comfort and confidence in effectively implementing inquiry learning. It is even fine to use more than one framework, if the patterns and commonalities between the processes are taught well; for instance, a school that normally prefers to use Big 6 in its English language arts classrooms may elect to shift to design thinking for a STEM-oriented community service project, and they can easily make that transition by helping learners crosswalk the two frameworks and understand why different vocabulary might be used in different contexts. The important thing is to use a framework, and to use it intentionally, deeply, and systematically, so that learners can fully understand the processes they are engaging in.

Collaboration will be a crucial strategy for the school librarian implementing inquiry learning. Not only will the school librarian need to collaborate with other educators on individual projects and lessons to effectively teach inquiry habits and processes, but they will also need to collaborate with their faculties to achieve buy-in to the concept of inquiry frameworks. It will be very difficult to implement inquiry learning effectively if the school librarian is the only person who understands and talks about the selected framework and processes. Ideally, all educators should be on board with the intent, stages, and vocabulary of inquiry so that they can plan for and reinforce it whenever a teachable moment to pursue the answer to a question emerges. Chances are excellent that most educators, including highly effective and experienced ones, have never heard of an inquiry framework. Even if they were college-educated in a content area that emphasizes independent research, like history or science, there is a high probability that the research instruction they received consisted largely of traditional procedures and formats (e.g., navigating periodical indexes or organizing notecards) rather than describing cognitive processes. Educators may need to actually experience a framework as learners by participating in an inquiry cycle, for instance by participating in a Professional Learning Community (PLC), in order to understand how to coach their learners through it. The selection of an inquiry framework may be most strongly driven by what classroom educators will believe in and adopt.

THE VALUE OF ITERATION

As discussed, inquiry is an inherently messy process! That cognitive mess comes from its iterative and recursive nature. There is no way to sanitize inquiry; to try is to turn it into a nice, neat, linear set of activities which might carry the label of "research" but really does not fulfill its promise for learning. Fortunately for us and our learners, Explore calls upon school librarians to embrace the mess of "iteratively responding to challenges" (AASL 2018, Learner and School Librarian V.D.1.). Despite many educators' established management habits, which tend to emphasize tidy and uniform work, there should be no need to eliminate the cognitive mess of inquiry when what we are explicitly called upon to teach our learners is to iterate, to go back and try again for further growth.

When we design instructional experiences, iteration can help us determine whether or not we have properly implemented inquiry. It acts as a helpful review, just as questioning assumptions does. If learners have no need to iterate, we know that there is something weak in our instructional design. If they don't run up against a challenge that they couldn't solve on the first try, then the inquiry didn't have enough meat to it; perhaps next time instruction should, for instance, include more in-depth topic exploration, so that learners have more chances to dig past the superficial and obvious facts. Similarly, if learners have no desire to iterate, something else needs to be adjusted in their experience; perhaps they need better support for question formulation to ensure they're inquiring about something that is authentically interesting and relevant to them, or perhaps educators' communication should be adjusted to model enthusiasm for iteration and to ensure the process does not reward simply finishing as quickly as possible.

Emphasizing iteration to our learners means that we have to show them that nothing worth doing is ever really done—there is always farther to push. This mindset is a learned habit, however, not an empty platitude that learners should be expected to embrace naturally. School librarians must explicitly teach and model strategies for pushing further: check another source, refine the question, refine the thesis, imagine it from another perspective, and so forth. Working in this way will demand an investment of instructional time, which can be hard for educators who feel pressured to cover broad content standards. However, if inquiry is to be attempted at all, there is no time *not* to allow for these things. To cut off iteration time is to render inquiry incapable of achieving its intent.

Dr. Carol Kuhlthau's research (1988) on the information search process (ISP), the underlying material for the Guided Inquiry Design framework, is especially pertinent when understanding how to guide learners through iteration. The ISP is an affective model, showing the emotional states that align with each stage of inquiry. The early stages of the model, particularly Exploration, which entails quite a bit of iteration, make clear that this work can feel confusing and frustrating. When frustration occurs, it's not because anything has gone wrong— that's what learning feels like! It is critical that school librarians teach learners (and other educators, as well) that those feelings are a normal part of the process—they only mean there is more to do. The solution is to lean in, iterate as needed, and push through the beautiful cognitive mess of an authentic inquiry experience.

Inquiry-Based Learning: Implementation Examples and Analysis

Everyday implementation of inquiry-based learning and the Explore Competencies and Alignments to which it's tightly connected can take a wide variety of forms in the school library. Following are several implementation examples, with each pair contrasting more and less effective executions of a similar idea, in the context of Explore's four Domains. The accompanying analysis notes are designed to help you understand what makes one example of practice stronger than another so that you'll be able to reflect on how their elements compare to your own practice and make decisions about some areas for professional growth you might like to pursue.

DOMAIN: THINK

Scenario: Your educator partners are interested in how to teach learners to think more critically about the opinions they hold.

Example A	Example B
• Invite learners to define the word *assumption*, generate a list of assumptions that they hold in their personal lives, and get in pairs and select an assumption that is important and interesting to them. • Assign them to debate teams in which partners will argue the opposite sides of the assumption they've selected. • Teach them to use a library database to gather information from at least three sources supporting both sides of the debate. • Hold the debates live in front of the class, and have other classmates vote on which side "won."	• Collaborate with a science educator to identify some of the common topical misconceptions learners enter with. • Open class with a multiple choice question to which many learners are likely to assume they know the answer—but don't reveal the solution yet. • Introduce several resources containing facts that challenge the assumptions inherent in that first response. • Engage learners in inquiry to gather information that will help them understand why their initial response might have been wrong or incomplete, and what assumptions were inherent in it.

Both of the examples attempt to teach learners to question assumptions. However, Example B authentically reveals learners' assumptions based on the opening question, challenges their misconceptions with conflicting resources, and then leads them to further inquiry to resolve that challenge. Example A, however, is focused on the debate activity and the database format use rather than focusing on actually questioning an assumption. At first glance, Example A might look more personally relevant because it is generated from learners ideas about topics, but it is actually less authentic because half the debaters have been externally assigned to argue against their own beliefs, and because success is judged by classmates' votes (likely based on stage presence or popularity) rather than deep reflective cognitive work.

DOMAIN: CREATE

Scenario: Learners are assigned to do research that will help solve a real-life problem.

Example A	Example B
• Learners start with a homework assignment to interview five people of any age in their neighborhood, asking what they love and what they find challenging about living there. • In class, they compare notes with other learners to look for common challenges that were brought up. • The school librarian conferences with learners to help accurately label the problems they've observed, then helps them use that vocabulary to identify search terms and appropriate resource types for their problems. • Some learners revise the problems they've identified after consulting sources. • Learners journal detailed notes about their findings so far, but then table their work to be continued after completing their next social studies and science class units, as those units will contain information that will help the learners propose possible solutions.	• Learners start by brainstorming problems that affect their neighborhoods. • Learners select a problem that seems personally meaningful, then brainstorm possible solutions. • Learners are given time in the school library to search books, databases, and websites for information in support of the solutions they've identified. • Each learner prepares a slideshow with a picture of their neighborhood, a description of the problem and solution they identified, and citations for each source they used, and presents it to the class.

Both of these examples start from the same premise of real-world problem solving. However, Example B assumes that learners already have the knowledge they need to both identify their real-world problems and to design solutions, with inquiry relegated to a confirmation activity as a late step toward the overall focus on creating a polished presentation. Example A, on the other hand, spends significant time on the cycle of design, with multiple inquiry activities starting early and informing every stage of learners' thinking. Example A does not bring learners to resolution like Example B does. However, Example A invests time in higher-quality problem identification; this is a positive end in its own right, as a stage of the design cycle, and it leaves the door open for an eventual return, which will yield possibilities for higher-quality solutions.

DOMAIN: SHARE

Scenario: A group of learners comes into the school library after working with their classroom educator to identify questions and topics about which they're curious, which grew out of what they've been reading in class.

Example A	**Example B**
• Learners need to research to find more information, so the school librarian delivers a short presentation reviewing what kinds of books are in the reference section, how to use the OPAC to search for books in the school library, and where to access the library databases on the school website. • As a reminder that their sources need to be high-quality and authoritative, the school librarian cheerfully announces "Remember, Google and Wikipedia are not allowed in here!" • When learners get stuck and can't find anything on their topics, the school librarian encourages them to think about their classwork again and choose a more suitable topic.	• To help learners start investigating how to find more information, the school librarian distributes copies of a simple flowchart she keeps handy, with guiding questions to help choose the right type of information source (e.g., Is your topic happening right now? Use a database to look for newspapers and magazines. Is your topic about how to do or fix something in everyday life? Search online for blog posts and YouTube videos.) • The school librarian circulates and provides feedback as learners work, guiding them to high-quality sources and additional keywords when they get stuck.

Both examples start with a presumption that the classroom educator has effectively guided learners to identify questions and topics of curiosity; because not all educators have this skill set, both examples could be improved by earlier collaboration with the school librarian. Once they arrive in the school library to begin their inquiry, Example A focuses on learners' compliant use of traditional source formats and ends up limiting some learners' ability to explore their interests. Example B, on the other hand, focuses on learners' choice-making about what type of source, traditional or otherwise, is best suited to the question or topic. Example B therefore allows learners more opportunities to engage their personal curiosity and co-construct how they will investigate it.

DOMAIN: GROW

Scenario: A school librarian and a collaborating educator want to implement an inquiry project, but they only have about three class periods available to dedicate to it.

Example A	Example B
• The school librarian and the classroom educator are careful to design an activity that learners will be able to complete successfully. • They ask learners to think about the topics they've been learning about and come prepared for class with topics they've chosen ahead of time, so that they can spend their library days searching a variety of sources, taking notes, and assembling their results in the written, oral, or visual format of their choice. • Regularly throughout the process, especially on the third day, the librarian reminds them to stay focused and use their time well so that they'll be able to get their products finished on time.	• The school librarian and the classroom educator decide to limit the scope of what they'll work through in this unit. • They issue learners a challenge based on some of the topics the class is learning about: If an environmental disaster were to end the world tomorrow, what should we save that would do the most good for the most people? • The first day, they let learners browse through a curated set of print and digital resources to start to formulate a thesis; the other two days, they help learners expand their search to additional sources. • For the last 15 minutes of each class, learners engage in peer conferences to challenge each other's thinking and provide feedback on gaps in what they've learned so far, then reflect on their search process and where they need to start again the next day. • Due to the limited time, learners simply turn in their refined theses, annotated source lists, and reflective notes, rather than developing a polished product.

Both of these examples show the school librarian and the classroom educator making the sensible decision to do fewer parts of the inquiry cycle in more depth, rather than trying to cram all stages into a short period of time. However, they have selected different parts to emphasize, and Example B is better aligned with the Explore Competencies under the Grow Domain. Example A emphasizes searching, analyzing sources for information, and managing time to develop a product at the end. (These emphases might be better aligned with some Competencies in the Inquire Shared Foundation.) Example B starts with responding to a specific challenge, rather than loosely picking a topic without guidance, as in Example A. Time is reserved in class for learners to provide each other feedback on how they're addressing that specific challenge and to reflect on their areas for growth and ways they might iterate and improve their search in those areas each day.

COMPASS CHECK

Questions for the Reflective Practitioner

1. Think about some of the recent inquiry projects that have been conducted in your school library, or that you have personally experienced as a learner. Which parts of the inquiry frameworks tend to be emphasized, and which are glossed over?
2. Envision the most exciting aha moments you have seen learners experience while digging into a topic they're curious about, or that you've experienced in one of your own pursuits at work or in your personal life. If you were to map those moments onto the inquiry frameworks, what stages would they likely fall into?
3. What are some ways you can use an inquiry framework to lead learners more intentionally and systematically into transformative moments of discovery?
4. What other stakeholders in your school community need to become active participants in designing effective inquiry experiences for learners? How might you open collaborative opportunities with those stakeholders?

5

Growth Mindset and Grit

During the spring and summer of 2020, the global COVID-19 pandemic was making educators nationwide face the ever more likely possibility of moving toward widespread virtual school for the first time. To say that most educators found this transition stressful is an understatement; so many felt the learning curve was so steep that it seemed as though everyone in the profession was in their first year of teaching again. Times of stress often make people seem to shed the more sophisticated layers of their personas and retreat to a raw state, revealing only a basic core that they can hold steady through the emotional maelstrom.

With those raw cores exposed, it became more possible than ever to observe a central difference in the ways people handle stress. Some became brittle, on the verge of shattering, experiencing the transition as a strike against their very identities as competent educators. Others deliberately leaned into learning their way through the challenge, absorbing professional development from all directions like a sponge, and committing to an open vision of what was possible for them to accomplish. The initial throes of virtual learning were not comfortable or elegant for anyone, but their patterns of stress response made a tremendous difference in the way educators perceived the transition. Those in the first group tended to see virtual learning as a pale substitute for their "real" jobs and an enormous burden of extra work to add to their plate, whereas those in the second group were more often able to feel hopeful about virtual learning's possibilities and envision ways they could use their new strategies to expand their practice even after the crisis was over.

All educators came to this field because they're interested in something about its outcomes—they just adore children and teens, or they believe an investment in young people will make the world a better place, or perhaps they benefited from an excellent educator and want to pay that experience forward. But when they arrived at the difficult situation of achieving those outcomes in a primarily virtual model, some thrived and others fled. The difference is not related to their talent, access to training, technological savvy, or experience. It's about their mindset and what they're willing to do to persist through challenges.

The response to professional learning under duress is an extreme example. But even under less challenging conditions, it is fairly easy to see a similar dichotomy in student learners' approaches to challenges. As a school librarian, when I assigned challenging inquiry units, some learners would get engrossed and say, "This is hard, but I'm working on something really interesting!" while others would just ask, "How much do we have to write?" When we taught learners to use a tool like iMovie, some groups would ask, "We know what we're going for, but we're not sure how to get there—can you help us?" while others would pick one group member and say, "You're the computer person, you do it." Some learners reacted to hard tasks by exerting effort and asking for help to improve. Others reacted by deciding it wasn't worth caring about, or trying to get out of it.

At the time, I thought these differences between learners boiled down to personality characteristics, rather than something that could be developed and purposefully built. But now it's clear that not only are growth mindset and grit teachable, they are also among the most significant indicators of learner success. The Shared Foundation of Explore calls on us to harness these ideas to create experiences that will help all our learners develop to their fullest potential.

In Your Backpack: Growth Mindset and Grit

Growth mindset and grit have been two of the buzziest buzzwords in education for the last few years. School librarians are more likely to have encountered these concepts from their school administrators, because principals and district leaders all over the country are looking hard at these concepts as possible frameworks for tackling the tough problems for which they're held accountable. And why wouldn't they? Growth mindset and grit are accessible to anyone from any socioeconomic background or demographic, and can be implemented for free under any school conditions. They have the potential to close gaps between subgroups by supporting learners who need to catch up while also accelerating high achievers. They are strongly correlated with growth and achievement, both in school performance and in career and life success far outside the classroom. And perhaps best of all, they are things that seem to be within an individual's control, appealing to many Americans' cultural sense of justice and responsibility.

Growth mindset is a concept that has been largely defined and popularized by the work of Stanford psychology professor Carol Dweck (2006). In a nutshell, *growth mindset* describes a person's belief that their intelligence is malleable and can be changed through hard work. It is in contrast to *fixed mindset,* the idea that we are each born with whatever capacity we get and that's that. A person's mindset probably won't reveal itself when everything is going well, but you'll be able to see it when they encounter a challenge. For instance, imagine you have a friend or colleague who recently bought a new computer and is frustrated with adjusting to a different operating system. Someone with a fixed mindset might use language like "I'm just no good at this—I'm really a PC person!" Someone with a growth mindset, however, is more likely to use language like "I haven't figured out the Mac yet, but I know I'll get there eventually. I just need a little more practice." The person with the fixed mindset has defined themself with a finite capacity, a skill set that is limited to PCs only, and thus sees their frustration with the new tool as somewhat permanent and out of their control. The person with the growth mindset, on the other hand, has defined themself with a capacity that can be built up regardless of where they started, and thus sees their frustration with the new tool as annoying but temporary. Both people experience the same challenges and learning curve, but one is prepared to conquer the obstacle and move on, while the other is ready to give up.

Grit is a separate but closely correlated quality that comes from the work of University of Pennsylvania psychology professor Angela Duckworth and set forth in her 2016 book *Grit: The Power of Passion and Perseverance.* Note the subtitle, because that's what grit boils down to: discovering your true passion, and putting in tremendous effort to pursue it even in the face of adversity. Both components are crucial. Passion on its own does not constitute grit; one can be intensely interested in, say, the ancient history of Egypt, but decline to study the subject when archaeology turns out to entail a lot of boring dirty work between rare massive discoveries. Nor does perseverance on its own constitute grit: if one pursues a career in law or medicine doggedly over a number of years because they thought it would come with a high salary or status, when they are in fact not actually interested in the field, then that's just opportunism or plain stubbornness. The magic happens when a person finds a field or topic to which they feel truly driven with a purpose, and when they are willing to pursue it to the best of their ability over a long period of time, regardless of obstacles.

HOW ARE GROWTH MINDSET AND GRIT DEVELOPED?

It is exceedingly important to understand that growth mindset and grit are learned and learnable qualities, not inborn traits—to believe otherwise would, in fact, very much indicate a fixed mindset! No person "is" growth or fixed; instead, they "have" one mindset or the other. Their mindset and level of grit may vary in degree, and they may shift some or display differently in various conditions. All people can learn to develop a growth mindset and grit, however, and can improve them with deliberate practice. For educators, that means that we can teach growth mindset and grit to learners, and that we must provide opportunities for them to engage in deliberate practice.

One crucial factor in developing these qualities in learners is employing patterns of praise as feedback. When we praise learners, we shape their thinking about what is valuable, important, and should be repeated or deepened. Not all praise is created equal! Some common forms of praise tend to describe the qualities of a learner's work: for example, "You've done an excellent job balancing multiple sources in this inquiry project." Educators often use praise to reinforce a learner's behavior: "I like the way you're sitting quietly and keeping your hands to yourself." Other forms of praise tend to describe qualities about a learner's effort: "I notice you've really been putting in extra hours and working hard to get this project done right!" Still other forms of praise tend to describe qualities about the learner: "Great job—you are really good at this!"

The latter two types of praise, and the difference between them, are critically important to the development of a growth mindset. When praise is about the learner, it contributes to a fixed mindset by describing positive qualities as something inherently gifted to them. In this fixed mindset, learners either have a strength in what they're doing or they don't, and they have no control over which areas are their strengths. When praise focuses on the learner's effort, however, it contributes to a growth mindset by describing positive qualities as something the learner has worked to develop. In this growth mindset, learners may not start with a strength for what they're doing, but it is well within their control to change their abilities through effortful practice.

To develop grit in learners, a crucial factor is creating an environment in which both rigorous expectations and warm support are strongly communicated. Perseverance cannot be learned by coasting through easy tasks that pose no difficulties! However, neither is it learned by getting mired hopelessly in impossible circumstances with no way out. It is learned and reinforced by facing a challenge and then surmounting it. To nurture perseverance in learners, we must continually set challenges for their performance—to solve complex academic or social problems, probe further into questions for deeper understanding, take risks to perform tasks that take them outside their comfort zones—while also supporting them every step of the way by ensuring they have the resources and the skills they need to come through those challenges successfully.

Another essential factor for developing grit in learners is that they must be able to make authentic choices about their pursuits. Passion rarely comes from another person's prescription or assignment. For learners to find their passions, they must have opportunities to be exposed to a variety of topics and options, with further opportunities to try what they like and practice it until they can achieve some level of mastery. This is excellent news for school libraries, which are among the best places in learners' lives for exploring a wide range of subject matter and discovering what appeals to them. When learners are able to choose a pursuit about which they truly feel passionate, and when they are then led to stick with it and continue working toward success even through challenges, that combination can lead to the powerful perseverance that has so much potential to make learners successful.

WHY GROWTH MINDSET AND GRIT MATTER

Imagine two 8th-graders from similar circumstances. Both are from middle-class families with college-educated parents. Each learner has access to the school supplies he needs, has parents who understand how to navigate the public school environment and expectations, goes home to a safe neighborhood, and faces no major socioeconomic barriers to success. Both boys are taking their first entry level algebra course this year, and both are starting to struggle. In terms of the factors most people associate with probabilities of success or failure—comfortable home lives, basic needs such as food and a safe environment, and parents who are involved but not smothering—both boys have equal odds of overcoming their difficulties in Algebra I. However, one boy shows signs of growth mindset and grit, and the other does not. How might their experiences play out differently?

The boy with the fixed mindset is likely to be flummoxed as to why he is having so much trouble in algebra. He's never had trouble in math before; his grades haven't been perfect, but they've come with a pretty steady stream of As, so people have always told him he's smart. Now that his test scores are frequently in the C range with an occasional D, he's starting to wonder if he isn't so smart after all. He used to like school pretty well, but now that he's feeling uncomfortable and less intelligent, he starts to lose enthusiasm. He can feel it in his history class, too; it's just too demanding compared to what he's used to. There's a flyer up in the hall for a student filmmaking competition, which he thinks sounds kind of cool, but it sounds like the sort of thing you'd have to be really good at to win, and he's not, so there doesn't seem to be much point getting excited about it. He plays it safe and counts on his easy science grades to get him into at least one good class when he starts high school next year.

The boy with the growth mindset, on the other hand, isn't sure why algebra seems so much harder than his previous math classes, but he's determined that if he could get As in those, then he can get an A in this one too. He just has to work a little harder at it. He didn't like receiving those first couple of Cs, so he decides he's going to need to try something new. He's always liked school pretty well, and he remembers a lesson the school's Student Success counselor did about study habits. He thought setting up a deliberate schedule for homework sounded lame at the time, but now that he needs it, he sees the value in that strategy and applies it to some of his other classes as well, especially his demanding history course. He sees the flyer in the hall for the student filmmaking competition, which is something he's never tried before but sounds super exciting and interesting. After some initial setbacks where he tries to film scenes of his friends outside but can't hear them well enough with his phone's camera and microphone, he decides he's going to need to learn more about filmmaking in general. So he uses the same technique that worked so well in algebra to set himself up a regular schedule for working on his movie project. Soon he's doing well in all of his courses and working on a filmmaking project that he's super proud of, regardless of how it does in the competition. It's a lot of work, but he loves it and feels great when he figures out how to get through each challenge. Plus, he knows he's setting himself up for his pick of the best honors classes when he gets to high school next year.

These two learners don't only have different results in their algebra classes. Their mindset and grit show up in their other courses, their extracurricular pursuits, and their general attitudes and enthusiasm levels. The boy with the fixed mindset suddenly is afraid he isn't smart, and becomes reluctant to take risks even when they sound interesting; the boy with the growth mindset, however, is willing to put in the work it takes to succeed, especially when it comes to his personal interests. The gap between them will only widen when they enter high school the following year, because the boy with the growth mindset and grit will start with better opportunities, lean into them with passion and perseverance, and turn those successes into still better opportunities in the future. The potential cumulative effect of this difference in approach is enormous, especially given the very similar circumstances the two learners started from. And because one of the biggest problems schools face today is closing gaps between groups of learners who do not come from such similar and relatively privileged backgrounds, it is easy to see why there is such increasing interest in teaching growth mindset and grit.

Growth mindset and grit have the potential to get kids through tough situations, whether they are academic, extracurricular, or social. They show potential for raising learners' expectations of what is possible for them to do with their lives by emphasizing hard work and perseverance as routes to achievement that are open to anyone who embraces them. The concepts are wholly egalitarian, available to any learner willing to put in effort, regardless of social class or station. They can be adopted at any time in a learner's life or career. And unlike many practices in school reform, growth mindset and grit lend themselves well to learning outside the classroom, by driving authentic interests and passions.

Growth Mindset and Grit in Explore

In the Shared Foundation of Explore, there are many close matches between the AASL Standards and the concepts of growth mindset and grit. In fact, some of them have used language directly from these areas of research! Explore's Key Commitment to "discover and innovate in a growth mindset developed through experience and reflection" (AASL 2018, 104) defines growth mindset as the necessary condition for the discovery learning that happens in school libraries. As learners experience an array of learning opportunities in our school libraries, whether it's through reading, research, using technology tools, or interacting purposefully with others, we are charged with helping them reflect on those experiences and adopt a mindset of "I can improve at this if I work hard at it." A closer look at Explore will show the direct connections between this Backpack item and the Competencies we seek to grow in learners.

SELF-ASSESSMENT AND EXPECTATIONS

Explore calls for "recognizing capabilities and skills that can be developed, improved, and expanded" (AASL 2018, Learner and School Librarian V.D.2.), which is exactly what Carol Dweck is calling for in her research. For a school librarian helping learners master this Competency, the most important operative word here is *recognize*. It is critically important that we develop tools for self-assessment and train learners to use them accurately. One cannot commit to growing stronger in any capability or skill if they do not understand where their abilities currently are. There are many possibilities for building self-assessment into our programming. Checklists, rubrics, proficiency scales, exemplars, online quizzes, conversation protocols, peer reviews—all kinds of tools, whether they're built specifically for the school library's purposes or a classroom tool that is used within the school library, can help learners recognize and understand how their current level of understanding or performance compares to what is possible. Then, once learners have engaged in self-assessment, they should be guided toward honest reflections about their level of mastery and areas for further growth. This reflection can happen in writing, through conversation, or a mixture of both.

In our role as instructional specialists, school librarians must maintain high expectations for learner performance. If we tend to expect little from our learners, it is unlikely we can help them develop a growth mindset, simply because a low bar does not leave much space to grow. How will we know if we have designed experiences that reflect high expectations? Simply put, we should be able to imagine any learner in our school completing the activity we've designed, and think through what kinds of feedback we might offer them to push harder and perform at a higher level. Chances are that if we look at an activity and cannot find a way to open it up for further growth for every learner, then that activity's design should be adjusted. For instance, if we have learners completing a genre-sorting worksheet that most learners can master and finish quickly, or perhaps older student learners are working through some sample web searches that have been designed with closed-ended right answers they can easily find and record, then we need to change the activity to something more challenging and open-ended! As an added bonus, not only are high expectations a strong teaching practice, they are an inclusive teaching practice. If everyone has room to grow, then no student is the only learner left behind.

MINDSET IN PROFESSIONAL GROWTH

As professional learners, school librarians must themselves adopt a growth mindset and grit. It can be hard for busy, experienced professionals to admit their vulnerabilities and identify the areas in which they need to grow. However, just as effective educators set high expectations for every learner, the AASL Standards set high expectations by asking each of us to "[embrace] new skills, knowledge, and standards in the profession" (AASL 2018, School Library V.D.3.), and we all have areas in which we can develop, improve, and expand our skill. Honest self-assessment and reflection on our practice, compared against Explore and the other Shared Foundations, will help us identify our strengths and our areas for growth (which may not be mutually exclusive).

In a profession in which many of us lack some of the resources we know are needed for best practices—adequate budgets, ample technology access, flexible schedules, paraprofessional support staff, and so forth—it is easy to assume that the areas where we need to grow are dependent on things that are out of our control. But remember that this sort of thinking, in which success depends on things we cannot control, is exactly the type of fixed mindset we are hoping to guide learners away from! As professionals practicing with a growth mindset, we must be determined to identify what we *can* control, and we must commit to the personal effort it will take to get our practice where we want it to be, by achieving what is described in the AASL Standards and which our learners deserve.

Happily, school librarians have many opportunities to learn and grow and embrace the endless stream of new skills, knowledge, and standards that the profession requires. Less happily, it is very difficult for many school librarians to do this, as all educators tend to feel pressed for time and overwhelmed by competing demands! Our growth mindset reminds us that it's less important to already know all these things and more important to be constantly moving toward them through our consistent learning efforts, however, and our grit reminds us that we are passionate about providing world-class school library services to our learners and our learning persistence is well worth the effort. With a growth mindset and grit in mind, we can read books (like this one!), monitor ideas and trends through social media, attend webinars and online courses, and collaborate with our peers to put our learning into practice. And when needed, we can adopt an action research approach (consider the structure included in the Boots section of this book) to seek out and invent new knowledge and solutions.

GROWING THROUGH PROFESSIONAL NETWORKS

School librarians have the opportunity not only to embrace their own growth mindsets and grit, but also to make those qualities communal with others by sharing through personal and professional learning networks. As leaders and collaborative partners, we are responsible for "modeling and promoting the use of personal and professional learning networks" (AASL 2018, School Library V.C.1.). These roles ask that we be brave and "start the party" by seeking out and inviting other like-minded professionals to form a network around a common interest, problem, or pursuit. This can be an exceptionally vulnerable effort in that it requires us to take the calculated risk of reaching out and starting a conversation or asking a question that no one may respond to. Because forming networks and collaborating are new habits for many professionals who in the past have felt obligated to display mastery of their field by appearing to already know everything, this can be sensitive and emotionally fraught even when the end result seems obviously beneficial.

Sometimes, in order to get past our sensitivity and hesitancy to find others who are brave enough to form a learning network, it is necessary to look beyond our usual circles and reach farther to find partners. Technology is an excellent method to do this; many school librarians and other professionals use blogging and social media as a means of extending their reach. That way, even if they haven't found other members of their tribe among their nearby associates, they can still build an effective network by reaching out to others across the country and around the world. AASL and other professional associations are also especially important for building our networks, as they allow us to make connections with other people by serving on committees, attending conferences, participating in virtual communication, and reading and analyzing professional literature.

At other times, however, the very best network may be our collaborative teaching partners within our buildings. As school librarians, we love to experience professional learning developed and delivered by our peers that is specifically targeted at librarianship. However, the proverbial rubber doesn't meet the road until that learning is brought back to our schools and put into practice with our learners, which is best done by figuring out implementation through collaboration with our classroom educator colleagues. Every idea we can gain from another school librarian will require some translation before it can be made to work in our own school libraries, with our own local conditions and constraints, and the other educators in our buildings are crucial partners in that translation. Sometimes the best learning happens when we get together with our building colleagues and create entirely new knowledge and ideas, simply by asking "why?" or "I wonder what would happen if..." and working together to tackle problems for which solutions don't yet exist.

MINDSETS FOR LIFELONG LEARNING

As school librarians we are called to build a growth mindset into the overall culture of our libraries. When we speak about lifelong learning, we're talking about something that is much bigger than any single lesson or program we offer in our school libraries. Rather, by "leading other educators and learners to embrace a growth mindset through lifelong learning"

(AASL 2018, School Library V.D.1.), it will become a habit to help all our stakeholders develop and practice within our school libraries and then carry these skills into the rest of their lives.

The large scale and import of this work demand not only isolated lessons or interactions, but also deliberate and ongoing connections between the present and the potential. Any time we invite younger learners to look at the work of older learners (e.g., through student art exhibits or living museum presentations or displays of inquiry projects), we show the younger learners a way to see growth as part of a continuum. They can learn to view learning as something more than what happens during a lesson, and to understand that problem solving is not merely something they can use to get past an immediate challenge, but a pattern of growth and grit that they can sustain as they grow older. We can also make these connections when we teach our learners to use resources, by always intentionally pairing the immediate need for the resource they're learning about (e.g., searching YouTube to find videos illustrating different views of a phenomenon they're studying in their science class) with reflections on what future lifelong learning needs they might also fulfill with that same resource (e.g., using YouTube to find videos illustrating different ways to solve a home repair problem). And of course, we can guide all kinds of conversations about reading into discussions about how books are a source of pleasure and new ideas not just now, but for the rest of our lives.

Promoting lifelong learning as a tenant of school library culture works beautifully when we feature role models. All members of our school and library communities can benefit from clear examples of what effective lifelong learning looks like. Showcasing what our principals are studying and learning about, for instance, can inspire a growth mindset among other educators by demonstrating that even our leaders are always striving to become better at their craft. Featuring the projects of parents or local professionals can give fresh inspiration to both children and adults about their long-term aspirations. Any time we can connect information in a lesson to a career, or incorporate an expert as one of our resources, we emphasize that learning is an ongoing way of becoming the kind of people we want to be, and that grit will turn our interests into our ways of life.

Growth Mindset and Grit: Implementation Examples and Analysis

Everyday implementation of growth mindset, grit, and the Explore Competencies and Alignments to which they're tightly connected can take a wide variety of forms in the school library. Following are several implementation examples, with each pair contrasting more and less effective executions of a similar idea, in the context of Explore's four Domains. The accompanying analysis notes are designed to help you understand what makes one example of practice stronger than another, so that you'll be able to reflect on how their elements compare to your own practice and make decisions about some areas for professional growth you might like to pursue.

DOMAIN: THINK

Scenario: You want the school library to be part of a schoolwide challenge to help young learners develop strategies for resilience and growth.

Example A	Example B
• Engage learners in a challenge that will require them to work in an unfamiliar and uncomfortable way, like switching from right to left hands to write or draw, or arranging a group of their peers in alphabetical order without speaking aloud. • Ask them to reflect on what was difficult about the task and what strategies they used to work past the challenges. • Then read aloud one or more stories about characters who struggle with achieving something, and ask them to look for places where the strategies they've identified might help those characters.	• Read aloud one or more stories about characters who struggle with achieving something. • Prompt learners: "Tell us about a time you struggled with something. How did you overcome the challenge?" • Allow learners to use art materials to illustrate the time they struggled and have them take their drawings home as a reminder.

Although Example B makes a connection to the abstract feeling of struggle and the need for growth mindset and grit, it does not require learners to actually experience or work past that feeling. Learners could respond to this prompt just by saying that most things come easily to them, or by inventing a response. Example A, on the other hand, has learners authentically identify solutions and then use the stories and characters to thoughtfully "practice" implementing those solutions. Example A will therefore be stronger for helping learners develop grit and growth mindset over time.

DOMAIN: CREATE

Scenario: One of your school's reasons for investing in a makerspace was the maker movement's promise of building self-direction and persistence among learners.

Example A	Example B
• During checkout time or when they've finished their assignment, allow learners to use the makerspace materials to make anything of their choice.	• When a learner asks a question about a demonstration they didn't understand in their science class, encourage them to use the makerspace materials to try it out and see what happens. • If they can't find materials to match the phenomenon they observed in class, coach their thinking on how they might be able to approximate the phenomenon using what's available.

Although both examples make use of makerspace materials, Example B shows better self-direction and more potential for learner ownership, persistence, and growth because it comes from a need to answer an authentic question. Example A may lead to those things, or it may simply be an enjoyable way to fill excess time after a lesson.

DOMAIN: SHARE

Scenario: Your district has strongly recommended that educators use Twitter as a professional learning resource, and you know your teachers will need help getting started.

Example A	Example B
• Offer a professional development (PD) workshop to other educators in your school community on how to use Twitter to connect with educators outside your school community. • The session includes setting up an account, searching hashtags to find and follow educators who post interesting ideas and articles, participating in a sample Twitter chat, and using mentions, replies, and retweets to start virtual conversations.	• Offer a PD workshop to other educators in your school community on how to use Twitter to get ideas for their classroom. • The session includes setting up an account, searching hashtags to find pictures that seem like they'd work in educators' classrooms, and retweeting articles so participants can find them easily in their Twitter feeds later.

Each of the examples addresses similar mechanics about how to navigate Twitter and offers a chance for other educators to learn something new. However, they have very different assumptions about why those educators would participate. Example B expects that educators will learn by passively consuming content. Example A, however, expects that educators will set up a meaningful network with two-way communication for continuous learning, and structures its practice activities with that type of use in mind.

DOMAIN: GROW

Scenario: You want to promote inquiry in your school as a way for learners to pursue their individual passions while growing their skills for self-directed learning.

Example A	Example B
• During an inquiry project in collaboration with a classroom educator, encourage learners to work hard and pursue their inquiry as deeply as possible. • Remind learners that they've been allowed to choose any topic they want to research, so this is their chance to learn something that will be important and interesting to them.	• Collaborate with a classroom educator to guide learners through small-group conferences to provide feedback about their inquiry projects. • Use a protocol such as a Charette or "Glows and Grows" to ensure that every learner receives both reinforcements and suggestions to improve their work. • After learners make revisions, repeat the process and prompt them to go deeper with their content and thinking.

Although both examples give learners the opportunity to improve and expand their skills, only Example B requires it. Example B's use of a protocol ensures that every learner is scaffolded to improve, regardless of their current achievement level, and will prompt the learners providing the feedback, as well as those presenting their projects, to think more deeply about the content. Multiple rounds of feedback will emphasize the iterative nature of developing expertise. Example A encourages learners to do these things, but assumes they already know how to do so on their own, instead of teaching the skills explicitly.

COMPASS CHECK

Questions for the Reflective Practitioner

1. What are some examples of growth and fixed mindset you've seen from your learners in the past? What about from your educator colleagues, or even yourself?

2. How do grit and growth mindset change the way your learners face challenges? What may be some of the impacts on their lives?

3. What are some ways you may be able to nurture growth mindset and grit as part of your school library programming?

6

The Maker Movement

As a district supervisor, many principals have asked me if their school library is supposed to have a makerspace. I always reply, "Only if it's going to be done the right way." The maker movement has swept the landscape of education blogs, conferences, and social media, but tremendous misunderstandings and disagreements exist about what implementation is really supposed to look like. Do you need to have a 3-D printer in a proper makerspace, or are paper towel tubes and pipe cleaners just as good? Does it have to be aligned to content standards to have a place in the school, or should we have a philosophical commitment that this is one place in the school where learners aren't subjected to rules and regulations? Do you have to have a flexible schedule to run a makerspace, or can you make it work within the bounds of a fixed rotation schedule, or do you really have to have a Genius Hour set aside? Are you allowed to issue design challenges to learners, or is it only a "real" makerspace if it's 100 percent open-ended? Opinions abound, and consensus is rare. This makes it awfully difficult for schools to decide whether makerspaces are worth investing limited funds to install.

My personal favorite example of makerspace programming in my district, so far, comes from South Knoxville Elementary. Viktoria Henderson, the school librarian who founded the school's makerspace, introduced it to her learners by issuing a challenge: "You're going to make a paper airplane fly as far as possible. You can use any resource on this table." The kids swarmed the table; returned to their seats with paper, scissors, and tape; and got busy building their prototypes. When all the model airplanes turned out pretty much the same, learners started asking Mrs. Henderson what to do next—but all she told them was "you can use any resource on this table." At that point, a few learners realized there were also books on the table, so they grabbed them and started looking through the pictures for new design ideas and directions about what to try next. There weren't quite enough books to go around, however, so some kids started to complain to Mrs. Henderson, whereupon she told them "I said, you can use any resource on this table." At that point, learners realized there were a couple of laptops on the table. Groups of them started crowding around, running Google searches to look for the best paper airplane designs. One learner saw a result that seemed promising but, fearing to break the long-established school rules, complained to Mrs. Henderson that he wished they could use YouTube videos. She asked him, "Is that a resource from the table?" He and his classmates brightened up and returned to work.

I love this makerspace example because it has very little to do with the materials used. Instead, the success of the activity depended entirely on learners' thinking and problem solving. Mrs. Henderson's role as school librarian was to coach learners, through questioning and feedback, to gradually deepen and extend their notions about what types of resources are valid and necessary to meet a need. In this way, the maker movement shows potential to teach learners a whole new way of approaching learning and exploration.

In Your Backpack: The Maker Movement

The basic idea of the maker movement is that we are born to make: it is our birthright. The very most natural way humans learn, just like any other animal, is first to play and then to solve problems, and the results of both play and solutions will be things that we have made. We are built to "just get in there" and try things, to create useful objects as well as beautiful ones, to take them apart and improve them, to use what we've made to buy from, sell to, and communicate with others, and eventually to leave them behind as artifacts for future people to discover and wonder about.

Another way to think about the maker movement is as something of a spin-off of "do it yourself" (DIY) culture. The DIY ethos is to learn to master skills, from food preparation to clothing production to home repair to car maintenance, on your own rather than depending on (and paying) others who have trained as experts. Doing it yourself demands that you learn and practice a wide variety of content knowledge and applied skills, and that you have the independent motivation to seek out that learning and practice it to achieve mastery. Being able to do something yourself is typically seen as a badge of honor—and this is not easy, as demonstrated by the prevalence of kits, how-to guides, tools, supplies, and television programs designed to make people feel they can indeed do it themselves. The maker movement combines DIY culture's persistence, independence, and broad-ranging skill sets with the assumption that learners will not merely develop the ability to do what others can do, but also begin to innovate and create in new and unique ways. Additionally, the maker movement aims to better connect people around the world by emphasizing that production of our possessions is not something that we should assume happens in faraway and invisible places, but something in which we all can and should be active participants.

Perhaps a better description, for those concerned about why schools should join the maker movement, is that makerspaces open doors for different types of learning, often informal, than those that tend to occur within traditional classrooms. The maker movement is aligned with constructivist learning theory because it is based on the assumption that we learn by doing something we know and then incorporating something we're not sure about, gradually expanding our use of tools and techniques and materials, until we gain deep knowledge and mastery through diverse hands-on experiences. The makerspace provides us with the opportunity to observe phenomena, and making gives us a way to build models and test hypotheses; it is well aligned with science for these reasons. However, it is stripped of the academic baggage that many find inaccessible, and instead emphasizes our innate curiosity, our need to try something and see what happens.

When learners participate in making, there is room for many so-called "soft" skills—the skills that increasingly are shown by research to have the most impact on learners' success in school and life—to emerge. As learners comb through tools and materials, compare notes with each other about what they're doing, and provide informal feedback and suggestions on what to do next, a highly authentic form of cooperative learning and collaboration emerges. When their project doesn't go right on the first try (or even when it does), learners have the room to try again and again, refining their work with each attempt, ultimately resulting in not only an improved product but also an important experience in grit and growth mindset. For some learners, the opportunity to make freely, see what happens, and decide their next steps might be among the most powerful opportunities for open-ended, creative problem solving that they will experience in school.

VARIATIONS OF MAKERSPACES

It can be difficult to define a makerspace with precision, and that is by design; the makerspace should have the capacity to become what it needs to be. As Diana Rendina, Colleen Graves, and Aaron Graves write, "a makerspace is not a room. It's a concept" (2017, 1). In their view, *any* space that cultivates participatory learning through maker culture is a makerspace—including the entirety of the school library, not just a set-aside area with fancy tools and supplies. For them, what makes the makerspace is the maker mindset. This way of conceiving the makerspace is an excellent match for blending the maker movement with the goals of the school and creating a unique solution for the local needs of its learners. However, it is a little frustrating for those who desire a concrete explanation of the shifts they will need to enact in order to implement making!

Fortunately for those folks, Graves, Graves, and Rendina do offer a much more concrete view of implementation, in which they recommend pairing makerspace with the idea of challenge-based learning (CBL). CBL starts by issuing a challenge to learners—ideally an authentic one, like a real-life problem they can design a solution for, or a group of people they can figure out how to help—and the makerspace provides a variety of tools they can use to build out their prototypes, tinker with, and improve. The selection of challenges can be tied neatly to big ideas or implications of classrooms' curriculum, and a variety of inquiry methods and content standards can be implemented in the course of learners' working through the challenge. As this inquiry deepens, the materials needed in the makerspace will likely include traditional print materials, online information resources, and crowdsourced or social media resources, all in service of learners investigating ways to meet the challenge. CBL-style makerspace use can be implemented within whole-class instruction or by individual learners based on the challenges they've independently identified as interests.

Other thought leaders advocate for minimizing the structured programming often associated with makerspaces so that opportunities are maximized for learners to self-direct as they tinker, play, and explore. In this view, casual and informal learning are highly valuable experiences that are often missing from other parts of the school, and the makerspace's role is to reestablish those opportunities in an environment from which, to the learners' detriment, they have been gradually squeezed out. Once those opportunities have been provided through the makerspace, the thinking is that a model of highly engaged and intrinsically motivated learning will emerge that translates into other areas of the school community. As Laura Fleming writes, though they are "quite elusive by nature and difficult to pin down, we should be nonetheless clear that informal learning opportunities for our students can inspire innovation and increase student performance in formal educational settings" (2015, 8).

Implementation, in this case, is less about programming and more about the creation of environment and culture. For this informal and unstructured view of school library use, the makerspace should be constructed to include a variety of tools for learners' use, with as few barriers as possible. Materials should be laid out and easily accessible, and learners should be encouraged to try using them in any way they want. This may include the simple production of "tchotchkes," which is not the ultimate learning goal. Like other types of open play, however, creating tchotchkes is seen as an essential step in exploration that will eventually lead toward more meaningful use and deeper learning. For this model to work, the culture surrounding the makerspace must encourage experimentation and failure. All educators with influence over how the makerspace is used must agree that undirected informal learning is a worthwhile long-term investment, because allowing learners time to casually tinker is inefficient for reaching goals in the short term, and it may take time for the desired innovative thinking to emerge.

Not all spaces associated with the maker movement are in school libraries or schools, or even defined as makerspaces—in fact, by most accounts, hackerspaces and Fab Labs were gaining popularity worldwide before the term makerspace was coined! These different types of spaces are similar in that they allow for open-ended tinkering and production among community members, but they do have slightly different emphases. Hackerspaces are typically understood to value the use of existing structures to do unexpected things, which includes tweaking products or processes to make them better or more useful (think "IKEA hacks" or "life hacking" as well as the more notorious computer hacking). Fab Labs are community spaces that allow fabrication and making, but they are "brand name" organizations that all subscribe to a common charter and have specific requirements about their spaces and tools. Pre-K–12 education has tended to gravitate mostly toward makerspaces in order to avoid association with the negative connotations often held by hacking and to maintain flexibility in planning, implementation, and funding.

Many schools and other learner-facing organizations were starting to implement tools, resources, and programming related to the maker movement before the term "makerspace" became part of the zeitgeist. For instance, the VEX Robotics Competition has been offering learners opportunities for tech-savvy making challenges since 2007. The programming language Scratch was released to the public by MIT the same year, and learning to code suddenly became accessible to even young children, instead of being a skill exclusive to industry professionals. President Obama's Educate to Innovate campaign, launched in 2009, included among its public-private partnerships the Maker Education Initiative's Maker Corps of volunteers to support young people in building and making. "Manufacturing Makerspaces," a February 2013 post on the *American Libraries'* website, offers a variety of examples of making as a means of increasing engagement in public and academic libraries, a trend that has also begun in school libraries.

In the end, each individual makerspace should be whatever it needs to be, and each school librarian should exercise freedom in building a space that meets the needs of their learners and school community. Based on her experience studying makerspaces around the world, Heather Moorefield-Lang writes, "This I can tell you: no two are the same" (2016). As with all programming and resources the school library offers its community, there are as many options and "right answers" for high-quality practice as there are schools and communities.

MAKING MAKERSPACES SUCCESSFUL

Any honest discussion of a still-emerging movement has to acknowledge the truth that not all implementations are equal. Although there are myriad options of "right answers," there are also some solutions that really just aren't right. It's important to keep this truth in mind when trying to establish a makerspace for the first time, because if early attempts don't go the way we'd like, we don't want to throw the proverbial baby out with the bathwater! The simplest and most common way makerspaces go awry is focusing on the stuff involved rather than the needs of learners. A stuff-first approach is highly likely to result in mismatches for the school community—not necessarily materials that are bad, but materials that are not right for that group of learners.

As school librarians, we know that we'd never try to develop a collection of print materials by buying books before considering what our readers want and need. Rather, we'd take a multipronged, ongoing approach to collection development, including steps like these:

- Weed the existing collection, to clear it of outdated items and clarify what valuable materials are already present.
- Take steps to improve access to existing materials (e.g., shifting shelves, adding displays, or updating signage).
- Solicit input from the school community through multiple channels, such as keeping a suggestion box, adding to an ongoing consideration file after collaborative conversations, or surveying learners and educators.
- Analyze the school's curriculum and current trends in materials use to look for needs that the school community might not be able to self-identify.
- Read reviews, from both the perspective of critics and the perspective of learners of the right age group.
- Promote newly acquired materials through announcements, displays, and formal and informal programming.

The same principles of collection development apply to makerspace materials. Before we buy a long list of popular products, we should follow a similar set of steps:

- Clarify what we already have access to, whether within the school library's walls or elsewhere in the school.
- Consider how those materials are currently accessed, and whether improvement is needed.
- Open a variety of communication channels to find out what our learners and educators are interested in exploring.
- Examine the school's curriculum for areas that learners or educators might not yet know could be better served by a makerspace.
- Read reviews and try products whenever possible, rather than blindly buying what someone else has.
- Plan to intentionally promote the new materials, remembering that learners and educators who haven't previously had access to them are unlikely to already know what to do with them.

In a paper presented at the ACRL Conference in 2017, Benjes-Small et al. summarized their research on what makes the difference between "Makerspace or Waste of Space" in their academic library. Although the specifics of implementation may look different in an academic library than in a school library, their recommendations contain valuable lessons about what will make or break the success of a makerspace:

- **Have a vision and purpose for the space.** The makerspace needs to have an intentional and articulated mission. We shouldn't create a makerspace just so we can say we have a makerspace; it should be helping us accomplish a specific goal. That vision and purpose will help us select resources to purchase, make programming decisions, and gain buy-in from the members of our school community.
- **Develop the space around need.** Needs assessment is a crucial and continual task throughout the process of planning and implementing a makerspace, and it first and foremost means assessing what needs the space will fill before selecting what equipment is needed. This helps us to use funding efficiently and make sure we're creating valuable opportunities for learners. The authors also recommend starting small with pilot programs so that future investments can incrementally build on what's already going well and shows clear alignments with community needs.
- **Have a supportive staffing model.** The makerspace can't fulfill its potential if nobody is able to pay attention to running it! School librarians rarely have the ability to hire or assign staff to a makerspace, but they can consider looking for motivated student workers to assist their peers with the resources, or forming tight collaborative relationships with other educators whose needs are aligned with the space. Time management may provide another route to help school librarians balance their work and make sure the makerspace doesn't lead to their own staff becoming exhausted. A planning conversation with a school administrator may help set priorities and guidelines for how much time should be invested in the makerspace each week, so that it neither falls off the radar nor cannibalizes other important duties.
- **Trust users and give them creative autonomy.** When learners are allowed to operate autonomously in the makerspace, they are more likely to develop a sense of ownership over the space and generate excitement about using it. If trust is not present, the hoped-for outcomes, such as learner innovation and creativity, are less likely to emerge.
- **Develop the space with and around community.** Strong relationships with learners, between learners, and with other educators are crucial to a makerspace's success. Trusting relationships are a precursor to the creative risk-taking desired in makerspaces, and they drive the culture of collaboration and peer feedback that we want to see in a successful implementation. Learners

who feel strongly related to the makerspace and the rest of the school library will become champions for these resources and advocates for them in the wider school community.

When looking at successful models, it's clear that thoughtful implementation is what makes the difference between a meaningful makerspace and a questionable craft corner, but it's also clear that being deliberately thoughtful is more important than the particulars of the implementation. In a complex venture like this, there is no substitute for continual planning, assessing, prototyping, and gathering feedback. As long as those processes are taking place, there are many ways a school library can participate in the maker movement. Making can happen on an individual basis in a flexible schedule, or on a whole-class basis in a fixed schedule. It can be mobile, with materials stored in carts that can move from the school library to any classroom or area that needs it. Schools can combine maker philosophy with other popular programming ideas like Genius Hour, 20 percent time, project-based learning, challenge-based learning, or Shark Tank presentations. It can be implemented through formal programming that may or may not be connected to the school library itself, like a technology class or a robotics club. As Laura Fleming (2015, 10) notes, the key distinction between the maker movement and other craft-centered activities is networking and social connections; that's what creates the participatory culture that leads to all of the positive outcomes we hope to see. And that means that whatever solution is the right fit for a school will be made possible by instruction and facilitation in those areas by a leader, like an effective school librarian, and not by the stuff itself.

The Maker Movement in Explore

The Shared Foundation of Explore includes several important connections with the ideas and goals of the maker movement. Appropriately, none of these connections are based on stuff! Instead, they represent the cognitive habits and skills makerspace proponents want all learners to develop, which can be embedded in a variety of aspects of a school librarian's practice. We'll take a closer look at Explore and how the AASL Standards call for us to embody the maker movement in our work.

CYCLES OF DESIGN AND INQUIRY

Many school librarians struggle with teaching cycles of design if they view Explore through the lens of traditional and print-based practices. If, however, school librarians view Explore with a lens that includes making as a means of deepening and extending the programming of the school library, design can be easily folded into how we view our broader inquiry instruction, and that gives us an effective route to implementation. "Problem solving through cycles of design, implementation, and reflection" (AASL 2018, Learner and School Librarian V.B.1.) is what the maker movement is all about, and strong maker programming will support learners to develop competency in these skills quite naturally.

Depending on the type of maker programming, this may or may not involve explicit instruction on design cycles and inquiry frameworks. As discussed, there are many ways to blend making into the school's curriculum, and some of them are informal and unstructured. However, as the school librarian guides and facilitates opportunities for making, those cycles and frameworks should always be in the back of her mind even if she is not delivering them explicitly to learners. The body of theory that delineates design cycles and inquiry frameworks is essential for ensuring that making, whether structured experiences or entirely informal, provides time and space for all of the cognitive processes that are needed to support learners in developing desired outcomes. Making is famous for leading learners to grow their soft skills, but the "soft" nature of those skills is exactly what makes them elusive in many environments. Design cycles and inquiry frameworks sharpen some of that softness and provide greater clarity on what work learners need to do to develop those skills. For that reason, they are invaluable tools for school librarians to use in ensuring that these spaces, materials, and activities are productive and the programming is worth the energy.

Facilitation of maker programming may include explicit instructional posters with rules or guidelines, or any other means of organizing those participating in the types of activities that hit the different stages of design and inquiry cycles. It might involve asking learners to exhibit their results, or to engage in feedback conferences at different stages of their work. It might simply involve a school librarian leaning over a learner's shoulder as they work on making something individually, and asking coaching questions to pull out learners' thinking through the various stages.

When a school librarian facilitates a making opportunity for learners, of all of the steps in a design or inquiry cycle, it is especially critical to ensure that time is provided for learners' reflection. Reflection is exceptionally important to learners' ability to gain solid problem-solving skills from their making experiences, as they thoughtfully consider what they've made, how it matches what they hoped or intended to make, what they'd like to change or improve in their next iteration, and how they might need to grow their skills to make that happen. Arguably, reflection may be the most important thing happening in a makerspace. However, it is also particularly tempting to skip reflection when time gets tight for learners—which, in a school, is all the time! School librarians play a critical role in designing making opportunities that will not squeeze reflection out of the timeline. For more detail on using frameworks to facilitate this type of cyclical problem solving, please see chapter 4, "Inquiry-Based Learning."

DEVELOPING PERSISTENCE THROUGH MAKING

When learners use a makerspace, the ideal is that they'll "[persist] through self-directed pursuits by tinkering and making" (AASL 2018, Learner V.B.2.), with the outcome that they'll develop deep-seated grit and determination which will prepare them for lifelong learning in any of their passions. As school librarians, we are accustomed to shouting from the proverbial mountaintop about building lifelong learners who have the skill set to independently pursue knowledge in school, in future careers, and in their personal lives. The fact that tinkering and making are designed to nurture those outcomes is glorious news for those of us who are worried about adding one more thing on our plate, because this Competency means making is not a new thing, but rather a powerful tool to accomplish something that is already among our core purposes.

A word of caution: there are many functions maker materials or activities can fulfill within a school library, but not all of them contribute equally to developing lifelong learners. Although some of these functions may have practical value in the short term, they are tangential to the actual goals of the school library and do not achieve the Competencies described in the Shared Foundation of Explore. At best, these tangential functions may seem like simple promotional efforts, or ways to get kids in the door, in which case the newly ensnared learners might at least stick around and partake in another resource. In a less-than-best case, these tangential functions may look more like reward time, an attempt at classroom management through extrinsic motivation, which is generally frowned upon. From a stakeholder perspective, there is a thin line between a makerspace and a messy time filler. A shallow implementation can end up distracting the school librarian from their core purposes rather than adding to them.

In order to accomplish our goal of developing persistence through self-directed pursuits, we need to ensure that while we're providing opportunities to tinker and make (AASL 2018, School Librarian V.B.2.), our focus is on learning rather than stuff. Activities and materials should always support the learning, not the other way around! If we focus on shiny toys or entertainment value or trying to fill time at the end of a lesson rotation, the implementation is destined for poor return on investment. However, if our attention is devoted to posing challenges that learners will need multiple attempts to overcome, or on supporting learners' inquiries by helping them model problems in order to see possible solutions more clearly, the implementation is much more likely to contribute to valuable outcomes like persistence.

As school librarians, we must design opportunities for tinkering and making with the same care that we would design high-quality lessons, even if those opportunities do not involve formal instruction. We must be intentional when thinking about what experiences will result in learners' active participation and exploration, and thoughtfully curate materials to support those experiences. We must consistently communicate expectations that learners are empowered to make decisions about what they make, but that the goal is to make, not to passively consume. We must commit to investing time and attention in conversations with learners about what they're making to engage them in thoughtful work and give them feedback that may lead to refinement or iteration. When we plan effectively in these ways, rather than simply purchasing stuff and assuming good things will happen, we can create a physical and digital environment that will support truly authentic self-directed learning.

MODELING PERSISTENCE

The most effective way for learners to acquire the behaviors we expect of them is to begin by modeling those behaviors ourselves. So if we want the outcome of our maker programming to be that learners develop persistence that will lead to lifelong learning, then we need to be deliberate and intentional about "modeling persistence through self-directed tinkering and making" (AASL 2018, School Librarian V.B.3.) as lifelong learners ourselves. It is not safe to assume that because we are good people and professionals this will happen naturally! Facing a learning challenge that requires persistence is an inherently vulnerable situation, and most humans' natural inclination is to cover up that vulnerability. Modeling it for our learners requires us to be brave enough to deliberately expose it and talk openly about it, labeling the weaknesses in what we're doing as well as the strategies we're going to use to strengthen our work.

The first step in modeling persistence is placing ourselves in a learning situation that requires it. This is our professional imperative to learn new things in public. It might include trying out new tools to create videos for our learners, attempting an innovative method for structuring lessons that educators on our faculty have been exposed to, tinkering with our own makerspace materials to improve the signage in our school libraries, or any variety of other things. All kinds of professional learning are fair game—except the kind that involves sitting passively in a workshop but then not changing our practice. The point is to try creating something new that stretches our skill set.

We need to display and talk about the rough edges on our first attempts. If we use a new tool to create videos, we might show a sample to a class and ask them what they like or would refine about that first attempt. If we attempt a new instructional strategy, maybe we could ask a collaborating educator for their feedback about how that strategy affected their learners' engagement. If we're trying to produce new signage for the school library, maybe we could mock up a sample and put it on display near where it will eventually be posted, along with a description of the tools and materials used and a comment box for refinement recommendations. Inviting conversations about unfinished work will make our learning process transparent and model it to others, and it will also give our school community a way to engage in our success.

After that, we iterate and refine our learning. Use the feedback to improve the videos, streamline the lesson plan, or polish the signage, then, if possible, go back to the people who provided feedback and thank them by showing them how their input contributed to your strengthened practice. If it takes multiple rounds of feedback and refinement to feel successful, then that's all the more opportunity for growth! Each conversation we have about something we're learning is a chance to model appropriate vulnerability and persistence. And the more learners we include in those conversations, the wider the audience that benefits from our model.

ENGAGING PERSONAL CURIOSITY

Engaging personal curiosity has been among school libraries' core purposes from their inception. Certainly, it is a fine and glorious thing to invite learners to pursue their passions with traditional resources. For instance, if our youngest learners are besotted with learning about animals, we have a chance to powerfully support their curiosity by pointing them toward books with high-quality photographs of puppies, marine life, and more. But widening our lens of practice to include the maker movement means we don't have to stop there.

"Fostering opportunities for learners to demonstrate personal curiosity and creation of knowledge through engaging with a wide variety of resources and technology" (AASL 2018, School Library V.A.2.) creates a professional playing field where all manner of resources can be considered valuable ways to nurture learners' personal passions. What if those same learners reading high-quality books could tinker with yarn and twine to fashion a leash for walking that puppy they're dreaming of, or a net to use in their bathtub or sink to role-play being a marine biologists who needs to collect and observe specimens? And what if they could use a simple app to program a character who explains their thinking on caring for those types of animals—describing how to responsibly train their puppy, or how good scientists make sure to return their specimens safely to the water?

Supporting curiosity with resources is something school librarians have always done, but the maker movement gives us many new resources to do it with. By incorporating all sorts of supplies and platforms for open-ended physical and digital production, school libraries become places where learners cannot only passionately consume knowledge, but equally passionately create it. This is not in opposition to our traditional promotion of reading and literacy; rather, it can support and strengthen it, by giving learners even more ways to engage with the ideas they encounter in books.

In the beginning, many learners won't be ready to create their own knowledge products, and that's okay. They weren't immediately ready to consume knowledge through reading, either! We teach and promote reading gradually and relentlessly over a period of years in order to support our learners in gaining skills and confidence, and we can teach and promote making in the same way. Our early implementation goals should be to create opportunities, remove barriers, and plant seeds so that learners' natural curiosities have the chance to blossom. Graves, Graves, and Rendina (2017) suggest using half-baked prototypes as strategy for this: when introducing a new material or technique, the school librarian tries it out as a learner would, and then puts their own amateur product out for student learners to engage with and improve upon. This half-baked prototype removes some of the barriers for entry to the new skill, allowing learners to immediately jump in to tinker and iterate rather than having to start from scratch.

In traditional practices we know that if we don't care for a particular book or genre, there is a good chance our taste will show up in our work with learners, and they won't read those things either, even though it might have been a much better fit for their own taste. That will happen with making, too. If we can't muster any personal curiosity or enthusiasm for tinkering and making, it will be hard to expect this type of programming to be worth much of an investment of resources. There is a good chance that if we try it and don't "get it," our intentionality for supporting curiosity is off. When that happens, we must always step back and adjust our view to make sure we're focusing on the experience of exploring and creating, rather than focusing on using the stuff. Doing otherwise, allowing ourselves to not like or believe in making, may make the whole implementation go awry and become a questionable use of time and funds. Just as with books, none of the materials in a makerspace will do anything positive for learners without a culture that promotes them and shows learners that they are worthy and participatory and exciting. But just as with books, devoting our personal energy to consistently promote and engage with making will invite learners into a world that can substantially enrich their lives and experiences.

The Maker Movement: Implementation Examples and Analysis

Everyday implementation of the maker movement and the Explore Competencies and Alignments to which it's tightly connected can take a wide variety of forms in the school library. Following are several implementation examples, with each pair contrasting more and less effective executions of a similar idea, in the context of Explore's four Domains. The accompanying analysis notes are designed to help you understand what makes one example of practice stronger than another so that you'll be able to reflect on how their elements compare to your own practice and make decisions about some areas for professional growth you might like to pursue.

DOMAIN: THINK

Scenario: After hearing that the AP Physics students have been building trebuchets, the school librarian believes all learners would benefit from trying their hands at building simple machines.

Example A	Example B
• The school librarian sets out varied materials and some pictures of simple machines to use as models, with the caveat that everything the learners build must be at a small enough scale to operate inside the school library. • As learners build prototypes and test them, the school librarian balances letting learners tinker and have fun with asking coaching questions about what they might be able to adjust to achieve better performance. • Only a few learners are brave enough to try this at first, but more join in as they see their peers' efforts. • The AP Physics educator collaborates by offering to spend a lunch period in the school library to answer learners' questions.	• The school librarian asks the Physics educator to collaborate on hosting a school-wide contest to use the principles of simple machines and makerspace materials to build tiny trebuchets that can be tested inside the school library. • The learner who can project a kernel of popcorn the farthest will win a fabulous prize from the principal. • Unsurprisingly, more learners initially sign up than eventually complete the contest. • An AP student ends up winning, applying the knowledge she gained from her Physics class.

In both examples, the school librarian tries to use their makerspace to extend access to a small group of learners' exciting and rigorous learning experience to the whole school. However, only Example A really creates an environment that fosters curiosity and using the resources for inquiry through tinkering and making. By promoting the project as a competition, Example B creates inequality in learners' participation and outcomes, incentivizing secret skill-building and eventually rewarding someone who already had special access to this knowledge. Example A is much more representative of the spirit of the maker movement, incentivizing peer mentorship, iterative improvements, and leaving the timeline open-ended for tinkering rather than cutting off exploration with an event date.

DOMAIN: CREATE

Scenario: Storage space is scarce in an old-fashioned elementary school library that's been retrofitted into a small former classroom area, so the school librarian has to get creative to implement a makerspace.

Example A	Example B
• The school librarian decides to clear off some of the shelving behind his desk to store the materials. • He has to weed his professional collection heavily, but that's fine because his educator partners prefer digital materials now. • His options to store supplies for repairing and processing new books end up pretty cramped, but it allows him to neatly store and label all of his maker supplies in plastic bins, so it's worth it. • He already has his learners well-trained not to go behind his desk for security reasons, so it is fairly easy to teach them to come ask him for any material they need to access for a project. • In the first few months he hasn't gotten many requests for the materials, but all the expert bloggers say demand will pick up soon.	• The school librarian decides to clear off some of the shelving near his instruction area. • He has to weed heavily in fiction, but his collection isn't evaluated by items-per-student anymore so it's fine to remove unused titles. • The shelf-shifting throws off his fiction signage, but he's been wanting to replace that with signage that incorporates the new maker resources seamlessly anyway, so it's worth it. • He makes plans to introduce the maker materials gradually during classes. • Learners can earn badges certifying they know how to use each product or tool, and after that they can access them freely from the shelves as needed. • It takes a few months for learners to get comfortable and confident, but then use starts to pick up.

Both examples show a school librarian who has to sacrifice something in their current arrangements in order to bring in maker materials, and who feels that the trade-off in space was well worth it. However, Example B is much stronger in establishing an environment conducive to independent exploration because it makes the materials accessible to learners without adult intercession and it includes instructional plans to make sure they know what is available to them and how to use it. Example A keeps the materials firmly behind an adults-only barrier and depends on learners to make requests, which they won't be prepared to do if they don't know what's back there. The passage of time may actually exacerbate this problem rather than help it, because as the novelty wears off, learners may lose some interest.

DOMAIN: SHARE

Scenario: Sixth grade science classes have been studying biomes and how environments influence animal adaptations.

Example A	**Example B**
• One learner who comes to the school library for book checkout with her English language arts class is thinking about her interest in the African savanna, so she tinkers with some of the maker materials to create a rough grasslands model while she waits for the rest of her class to finish checking out books. • The school librarian notices what the learner has done and asks her to explain more about it. • The learner points out the different animals she's drawn and molded out of clay (depending on what colors were handy) and mentions that she's still uncomfortable wondering how all these prey species can live right alongside the big famous predators without getting eaten immediately. • The school librarian knows that the local zoo's outreach department is friendly and generous to schools, so she suggests that they send a picture of the model over to a zoo biologist and ask for feedback on her question. • The zoo responds a few days later and compliments the learner's thinking but uses her model to gently correct her misconception about the scale of the savannah and how closely animals live.	• The school librarian is eager to use her new makerspace to collaborate with educators and generate interest in the materials, so she suggests to the science department that after they cover the content in their classrooms, they can bring their classes to make models of each type of biome. • The science educators split their learners into groups and assign each a biome to illustrate on a large poster. • There is a parent-teacher conference event coming up soon, so these posters will make perfect promotional items to hang in the hallway as evidence of the fun and engaging work families can ask their learners about. • The school librarian doesn't always have many requests for conferences during these events, so she looks forward to the opportunity to stand in the halls near the posters and start some conversations with families about how they can get involved as volunteers in the school library.

In each of these examples, the makerspace is intended to support the learning happening in science classes and encourage members of the community to participate in school library activities. However, Example A is a much stronger implementation of the Explore Competencies, even though it only involves a single individual learner versus a whole grade level's classes. In Example A, a learner uses found time to explore a self-directed interest through tinkering, the school librarian coaches the learner on how to seek further feedback to expand her science content knowledge, the model she's made serves as a vehicle to illustrate and later fill the gaps in her thinking, and a community member with a real connection to her question is consulted. In Example B, learners have no choice about what they're making; the poster activity is misaligned with the learning targets, acting merely as a flashy arts-and-crafts project for decorative purposes rather than deepening or reinforcing the science content, and the anticipated community conversations are tangential to the learning work at hand.

DOMAIN: GROW

Scenario: A school librarian who's never tried implementing a makerspace before has an aha moment over the summer break.

Example A	Example B
• A school librarian rarely has access to travel funding to attend conferences, so she is exceptionally excited when her state affiliate association offers a summer professional development day near enough that she can do it as a day trip. • One of the sessions there is about another school librarian's experience funding a makerspace with grant money. The librarian has never encountered the maker movement before, but she immediately gets excited and thinks this is the perfect opportunity to help her community see the school library as exciting and relevant. • She starts making plans to ask her parent-teacher organization for a 3-D printer, and asks the presenter to make sure she's getting a good brand. • In the fall, she buys a makerspace kit one of the major vendors was advertising; it takes more of her budget than she wanted to spend, but it saves her the time of researching all the individual products, which she's way too busy to do. • The summer presenter had been very encouraging about letting the kids figure out the tools and teach each other, so when the kit arrives, the school librarian just puts it out on a table and waits for the magic to happen. • She keeps meaning to play with the tools herself when she gets a chance, but school life is so busy, there's always something else to do.	• A school librarian has a leaky faucet in her home. When working through an online search for a trustworthy plumber, she notices that many of the search results are for how-to videos on YouTube showing how anyone can fix a simple leak. • It dawns on her that learners could be significantly empowered if they realized how many instructional videos were at their fingertips, and if they had access to a few common tools so they could dig in and try things. • She chats with a few stakeholders, who love the idea of a space where learners can practice independence and "adulting." • She hasn't been able to afford conference travel for a long time, but when her state affiliate association offers a summer professional development day near enough that she can go, she attends a session on makerspaces and realizes that's exactly the body of work she needs to draw on. • She does a little more research about makerspaces, then goes to her parent-teacher organization (PTO) to describe her vision and ask for help funding it. • The PTO doesn't think the 3-D printer the summer presenter mentioned will help their kids much, but they love the idea of asking families to donate tools and supplies that all learners can access for a variety of projects. • The school librarian is excited to become more "handy" and learn alongside her learners.

Both of these examples result in efforts by school librarians to implement makerspaces. Neither is very confident with their knowledge about the maker movement, but each was able to access timely summer professional development on that topic and took action to follow up on their learning. However, Example B is a much stronger example of a school librarian embracing new skills and knowledge in the profession as they relate to teaching and learning. In Example A, the school librarian is primarily trying to solve problems of money and appearances; she thinks investing in this programming will create a perception that her school library is innovative, so she starts asking for funds and buying equipment without much thought about assessing the real needs of her learners. In Example B, however, the school librarian uses a personal experience to identify an unmet learning need in her community, then speaks with stakeholders to assess and find funding to serve that need, using the makerspace professional development as a framework to guide her local community-based efforts. Example A never goes beyond the stuff, but Example B begins with the school librarian embracing how her new knowledge can create experiences that truly impact a learning need.

COMPASS CHECK

Questions for the Reflective Practitioner

1. Which of the learners in your own school library might be well served by the goals of the maker movement?
2. What might be some ways that expanding our definition of "resources" could impact learners' experiences in the school library?
3. What are some steps that might help you assess your school community's needs related to making?

7

Personalized Learning

During my time as a high school librarian, I had the privilege of working with a cohort of particularly delightful teenagers. These young people were everything we'd like our own children to be: intelligent, creative, compassionate toward others, willing to put in hard work toward causes that matter, funny (okay, *really* funny), and so forth. As learners, these kids were truly the cream of the crop.

And so they made an interesting case study when looking at instructional strategies in my school, because we could see them as something of an ideal case. If something wasn't working for that group of learners, then it should be easy to diagnose that it wasn't going to work for anybody. Consider two experiences this group had:

- As freshmen, these learners were part of the annual National History Day (NHD) competition that our team-teaching Honors English and Honors World History educators used to organize some of their curriculum. Within the parameters of the competition, these learners got to choose a topic for inquiry and work on it throughout the year. They had flexible assignments to guide their research skills development along the way, and they had choices about the product they'd create to demonstrate their learning. An additional process paper ensured that reflection and metacognition supported their learning journey. They were hugely successful, both in their classroom learning goals and in moving forward in the competition.
- As juniors and seniors, these learners were the first at their school to write Extended Essays (EEs) for International Baccalaureate diplomas. The new EE experience, an eighteen-month research arc with choice of topics that echoed and deepened classroom learning, had much in common with the established NHD experience. But learners' success level was not similar.

> Many selected topics they did not like, struggled for motivation to make progress, became distressed at the wide-open nature of the task, and turned in shallow work at the last minute.

Why the difference in results between two open-ended inquiry experiences? I believe it came down to an unfair assumption that, as upperclassmen, these students were prepared to act independently as expert learners, when in fact they needed some supports. The NHD competition had those supports built into the coursework, but the EE did not. Being born brilliant was not enough to make these learners successful—and it's certainly not enough when we think about extending these rich opportunities to a larger proportion of the school community.

The principles of personalized learning provide routes for all students to become expert learners so that they can successfully tackle ambitious work that they choose and believe in. Personalization puts learners in the driver's seat to take charge of their experience—but it does not just pull the rug out from under them, leave them to fend for themselves, and hope they make good choices. Nor does it negate the crucial importance of the educator guiding and supporting them. Instead, personalized learning thoughtfully supports learners in acquiring the skills they need to set goals, design work products, build a network of supportive peers and coaches, and connect learning with their personal passions. Personalization leads learners toward authentic ownership of everything they will explore in school and life.

In Your Backpack: Personalized Learning

Personalized learning, in a nutshell, is a way of thinking about how to create experiences that put learners in charge of their own education. Personalized learning environments (PLEs) do not consist of programs or methods or tools, but instead represent a philosophical foundation to how all learning experiences are constructed. Personalization is not only one thing, nor even necessarily a new thing. It assembles learning theories all the way back to the educational psychology canon of child-centered education and social constructivism by John Dewey, Lev Vygotsky, and Jerome Bruner, as well as more recent work on flow and mindset by Mihaly Csikszentmihalyi and Carol Dweck (see chapter 5). Its defining characteristic is that it is centered on learners, their needs, and their interests.

As a simple matter of vocabulary, personalization is often confused with differentiation and individualization. All three imply that learning should be tailored to what each learner needs, rather than treating them all the same. The difference is in who is doing the tailoring (figure 7.1). Differentiation and individualization are both teacher-centered. In differentiation, educators divide their learners into small groups and tailor instruction to those groups' needs. In individualization, educators treat each learner differently according to their needs—but in both cases, all of the decisions about learner differences are made by the educator. In contrast,

There is a difference between personalization, differentiation, and individualization. One is learner-centered; the others are teacher-centered.

PERSONALIZATION	DIFFERENTIATION	INDIVIDUALIZATION
The Learner . . .	**The Teacher . . .**	**The Teacher . . .**
drives their learning.	provides instruction to groups of learners.	provides instruction to an individual learner.
connects learning with interests, talents, passions, and aspirations.	adjusts learning needs for groups of learners.	accommodates learning needs for the individual learner.
actively participates in the design of their learning.	designs instruction based on the learning needs of different groups of learners.	customizes instruction based on the learning needs of the individual learner.
owns and is responsible for their learning that includes their voice and choice on how and what they learn.	is responsible for a variety of instruction for different groups of learners.	is responsible for modifying instruction based on the needs of the individual learner.
identifies goals for their learning plan and benchmarks as they progress along their learning path with guidance from teacher.	identifies the same objectives for different groups of learners as they do for the whole class.	identifies the same objectives for all learners with specific objectives for individuals who receive one-on-one support.
acquires the skills to select and use the appropriate technology and resources to support and enhance their learning.	selects technology and resources to support the learning needs of different groups of learners.	selects technology and resources to support the learning needs of the individual learner.
builds a network of peers, experts, and teachers to guide and support their learning.	supports groups of learners who are reliant on them for their learning.	understands the individual learner is dependent on them to support their learning.
demonstrates mastery of content in a competency-based system.	monitors learning based on Carnegie unit (seat time) and grade level.	monitors learning based on Carnegie unit (seat time) and grade level.
becomes a self-directed, expert learner who monitors progress and reflects on learning based on mastery of content and skills.	uses data and assessments to modify instruction for groups of learners and provides feedback to individual learners to advance learning.	uses data and assessments to measure progress of what the individual learner learned and did not learn to decide next steps in their learning.
Assessment **AS** and **FOR** Learning with minimal **OF** Learning	Assessment **OF** and **FOR** Learning	Assessment **OF** Learning

FIGURE 7.1 /
Personalization versus Differentiation versus Individualization Chart

in personalized learning, we work toward a state in which learners can make their own decisions about their individual needs. *Work toward* is operative, here: there is obviously a continuum of learners' abilities to make mature and high-quality decisions, and there will be times when educators need to press in more closely because learners are not yet equipped to handle autonomy. But when we make progress toward that end, we are heading toward a vision of exploratory learning that will result in better served, more motivated, more interested, and just plain happier learners.

UNDERSTANDING PERSONALIZATION VIA COUNTEREXAMPLE

It may be easiest to begin to understand personalization by first thinking about what it is not. Picture the typical teacher-centered classroom: The educator is wholly in charge of what happens in every lesson, every day. For many experienced educators, this does not seem like a bad thing on its face—because what's the alternative? Allow children to run amok with no rules and let chaos reign? The mistake here, perpetuated by decades of inadequately funded schools, is that many educators have historically been forced to conflate instruction with supervision and classroom management. A lack of resources to do otherwise has created a system in which keeping learners physically safe and orderly has meant keeping the educator in control of everything.

But when the educator has all the control, that necessarily means the learners have no control. It means they are passive. And since we know that the empty-vessel model of learning is wrong, we also know that passive learners don't do much learning. We cannot pour knowledge into brains; our learners have to actively construct it. So because our need for supervisional control (i.e., our practical need to keep learners' wiggly bodies and loud mouths safe and under wraps) has ended up deeply coupled with instructional control, such that learners have few routes to active construction, we have ultimately designed a system that we know won't result in learning.

Instead, it results in the stereotypical passive learners that make passionate and optimistic educators feel dragged down and disappointed in their careers: zombie students who only want to know whether a given factoid will be on the test, identical work submissions that show compliance and parroting rather than any actual thinking, grades and feedback that learners don't seem to understand or care about, and petulant daily whines of "why are we doing this?" Anyone who has spent time with a very small child knows that learners do not start out as passive zombies. On the contrary, they start out wildly curious and self-motivated and eager to explore! We often lament that they lose those qualities as they get older, but that simply isn't true. We can see older learners express their intrinsic drive for learning when they voluntarily sink their whole minds and work ethics into mastering video games, sports and dance, arts and music, or any number of other extracurricular pursuits.

When we don't see this in schools, it's because we have systematically suppressed it by making learners passive.

Clearly, *no* educator wants this outcome. In fact, most of us are devastated by it. But all of us tend to teach the way we were taught, and we were by and large taught in teacher-centered classrooms, so we unwittingly perpetuate it. Many of us desperately want to create different outcomes for the learners in our care, but we lack the supports and resources and models to envision a different way of doing business. And, after all, we *do* still have the paramount obligation to keep our learners safe while they are with us. So how's a caring educator to confront this conundrum?

Personalized learning puts the learner back at the center of the classroom, while still keeping learners safe, by uncoupling instructional decision-making from supervisional decision-making. Adults still need to captain the big-picture concerns of keeping schools orderly and functional, but even our youngest learners can start developing their abilities to become active learners and make appropriate educational decisions when we carefully coach them toward that end. And our older learners desperately need the opportunity to start honing their abilities to learn autonomously, because they'll have no choice once they graduate and move on to their next stages of college, career, and life. Personalization gives us a route away from the old, systematically passive learning, in order to develop a new system of active learning and learner ownership.

Admittedly, the old system works fine for some learners. It is not fair to claim that no learners have been well served by teacher-centered classrooms, or that all learners have succumbed to the passive zombie stereotypes. Clearly that is not true; all educators can point to examples of particularly bright, curious, self-motivated learners who have had tremendously positive outcomes in traditional school settings. But personalization argues that *all* learners have the innate potential to be curious and self-motivated, that they *all* deserve those positive outcomes, and that it is our responsibility as educators to create learner-centered environments to make that possible.

CREATING PERSONALIZED LEARNING ENVIRONMENTS

Now that we're clear on how personalized learning pushes back against the old system of teacher-centered environments, let's explore how to actually work toward a new system of learner-centered environments. As mentioned earlier, personalized learning environments (PLEs) are not simple programs or tools, nor do they comprise only one set of actions or look one single way. However, they do have some common characteristics that educators can use to start shifting control and decision-making to their learners. These PLE characteristics are designed to support learners in developing the skills they need to thoughtfully seek new knowledge, monitor their progress, and build learning networks with their peers. Although no comprehensive list exists (again, because PLE is not just one thing nor the work of just one researcher), the following elements make an excellent starting point for considering some ways to shift one's practice toward personalization:

- Learner profiles
- Goal-setting
- Standards-based assessment
- Success criteria

Learner profiles are an essential structure in PLE for learners to develop self-knowledge. Formats for learner profiles can range widely (e.g., slideshows, portfolios, posters, cover sheets in notebooks, even a simple conversation in which the learner talks and another person takes notes), but whatever they look like, they should assemble information about the learner as an individual. This information might include personality traits, strengths, weaknesses, interests, learning preferences, environment preferences, passions, culture, or any other descriptions of what learners know or can come to know about themselves. It can even include academic information, such as an inventory of what content standards within a class a learner has already mastered and which ones still need growth. The profile can be dynamic, with learners gradually adding to or revising it throughout a course or school year. The key to making this exercise learner-centered is that it must be the learner who gathers and uses this information, not the educator. Certainly, the educator can benefit from knowledge gained through a learner profile, but the driver of this exercise should be the learner.

Centered in the self-knowledge gained from their learner profiles, learners can participate in rigorous goal setting. In the context of PLE, this is different from the goals often observed in the classroom. Goals shouldn't be too large or distant to truly envision ("my goal is to play for the NBA"), nor tangential to the work of the classroom ("my goal is to earn enough money to go on a trip this summer"). Although learners may certainly be encouraged to have these types of dreams and aspirations, personalized learning calls for them to set goals that define the direction of their learning. In this way, learners are given a central measure of power and decision-making in their academic work.

Learners' goals should be supported by a philosophy of standards-based assessment. Standards-based assessment practices measure learners' mastery of the content standards, rather than averaging their performance on assignments, as in traditional grading practices. In standards-based assessment, retakes and revisions are not penalized, because they show how learners are growing toward mastery. Multiple representations of learning are valid, and learners have room to exercise choice and voice in the formats they use to represent their mastery. Summative grades are based on recent work, rather than averaging all work, as it is assumed that early work will show less mastery and therefore shouldn't weigh down a final assessment. Extra credit is not necessary, as anything and everything that moves learners toward mastery is just "credit," and behavior is either not graded or is separated from assessments of learning. These shifts in how we measure success in learning are powerful for creating learner-centered experiences because they allow flexibility for learners to identify and work on their personal areas where growth is needed, rather than moving in lock step with the group.

Success criteria are a high-leverage strategy to support both goal setting and standards-based assessment. Essentially, what they do is clearly define what mastery of a learning objective looks like—and they do it right up front when a unit is introduced, rather than being kept secret until the end as in many traditional practices. For learners to be able to set and achieve goals for mastery, they need to know what mastery will entail. When they have clear success criteria, they not only begin to drive their path to success, but they can also learn to monitor their own progress and adjust their approaches as needed.

Over time and with deliberate practice, the use of measures like these will support learners in developing the habits and mindsets of expert learners. Learner profiles help them understand their strengths and passions so they can make choices that are good fits; goal setting helps them connect their self-knowledge to the curriculum; standards-based assessment creates the safety for learning that isn't perfect the first time and the flexibility for multiple ways to demonstrate learning; success criteria help them define mastery and monitor their progress. All of these elements support learners who are beginning to drive their own experiences so that educators can begin to turn over some control without creating chaos in the classroom.

CHANGING ROLE OF THE EDUCATOR

The shift to learner-centered instruction comes with necessary shifts in professional practice that many educators will find a relief, once they can envision them—but these shifts may be hard to envision at first, because most of us have had little opportunity to witness those shifts in our own experiences as learners. The need to move "from sage on the stage to guide on the side" has often been promoted in professional development settings, but that advice is difficult to follow when it comes from lecturers who are quite literally on the stage in large auditoriums! Here we'll talk about some more concrete ways of actually transitioning elements of control and ownership over to learners.

Barbara Bray and Kathleen McClaskey, consultants and specialists in personalization, describe three stages of PLE (2015, 75–77). These stages paint a more detailed picture of what the phases of transition from teacher-centered to learner-driven classrooms might look like (figure 7.2).

- Stage One keeps the educator in control but encourages more learner choice and voice during tasks.
- Stage Two positions the educator and the learner as partners in co-designing learning experiences.
- Stage Three is when the learner is equipped to take the lead.

STAGE ONE TEACHER-CENTERED	STAGE TWO LEARNER-CENTERED	STAGE THREE LEARNER-DRIVEN
The teacher . . .	**The learner . . .**	**The learner . . .**
understands how each learner learns based on Learner Profile (LP) and data.	with teacher guidance updates LP by recognizing how learning changes.	monitors and adjusts LP as he or she learns with teacher as a partner in learning.
makes instructional decisions on methods and materials based on four diverse learners' LPs to create a Class Learning Snapshot (CLS).	identifies learning strategies and skills with teacher to create action steps for learning goals in PLP.	is an expert learner with agency who applies innovative strategies and skills to redesign and achieve learning goals in PLP.
refers to CLS to redesign learning environment by changing physical layout of classroom.	co-designs the learning environment with multiple learning zones with teacher.	expands the learning environment in and outside of school to include the local and global community.
universally designs instructional methods and materials and guides learners to establish learning goals in Personal Learning Plan (PLP).	with teacher decides how he or she accesses information, engages with content and expresses what they know using learning goals in PLP.	self-directs how, when, and where he or she achieves, monitors, and adjusts learning goals in PLP.
revises lessons and projects that encourage learner voice and choice.	and teacher are transforming lessons and projects together to include learner voice and choice.	designs challenging learning experiences based on interests, aspirations, passion, and talents.
designs activities to include tools and strategies that effectively instruct and engage all learners in the classroom.	with teacher acquires skills to choose and use the appropriate tools and strategies to access information, engage with content, and express what he or she knows and understands.	independently applies tools and strategies so he or she can explore deeper and challenging experiences that extend learning and thinking.
is introduced to competency-based learning. Learning may be part of a standards-driven, time-based grade level system.	demonstrates mastery of learning standards that may or may not be in a grade-level system transitioning to or are in a competency-based system.	learns at his or her own pace and demonstrates mastery with evidence of learning in a competency-based system.

FIGURE 7.2 / **Stages of personalized learning environments**

STAGE ONE TEACHER-CENTERED	STAGE TWO LEARNER-CENTERED	STAGE THREE LEARNER-DRIVEN
The teacher . . .	**The learner . . .**	**The learner . . .**
or counselor suggests after-school and extra-curricular activities to learners based on learning goals in PLPs.	and teacher work together to determine extended learning opportunities (ELOs) based on college, career, personal and citizenship goals in PLP.	self-selects ELOs based on college, career, personal and citizenship goals as well as his or her interests, aspirations, passion, and purpose.
uses or adapts existing formative and summative assessment strategies and leads learner conferences with parents.	contributes to design of peer and self-assessment strategies, reflects on learning, and leads conferences with parents, teachers, and peers.	designs assessment and showcases evidence of learning through exhibitions that involve parents, peers, teachers, and community.

These stages help flesh out what it means for the educator's role to become facilitator, coach, and partner to learners.

The three stages of PLE also make clear that in order to progress from one to the next, learners will need to develop some skills they may not currently have developed in their traditional classroom environments, which will prepare them to effectively manage their increasing responsibility and autonomy. Think back to the narrative that opened this chapter—learners, even brilliant, hard-working young adults, cannot spontaneously display the skills needed to function autonomously in PLE without supports. A major role of the educator is to organize instruction to teach those skills along with teaching content, gradually releasing control as learners are able to become more independent.

Structures and routines are key to gradually developing the skills that expert learners need. Educators are already well accustomed to building classroom management structures and routines, and that same pattern of practice established for supervisional needs can be applied to serve instructional needs. The thinking routines published by Harvard's Project Zero are an excellent place to start: these are simple structures, based on high-quality research, to help learners develop the thinking dispositions and competencies they'll need for driving their own learning and monitoring their progress. Kagan cooperative learning structures, when used in the context of a learner-centered classroom, can be effective routines for facilitating and expressing learner voice (Clowes 2011). The inquiry frameworks discussed in chapter 4 of this book are another way to provide structural support for allowing learner choice and guiding its pursuit.

It will take time, for both learners and educators, to develop these skills and move through the PLE stages. In *A Handbook for Personalized Competency-Based Education,* researcher Robert Marzano and his colleagues suggest a scope and sequence for teaching and reinforcing both cognitive and metacognitive skills, spreading these skills across the grade levels and content areas with which they best fit (Marzano et al. 2017, 19–24). The happy news is that by using these sequences, no educator needs to attempt to enact personalized learning on their own! PLE can and should be a collaborative effort, with professional learning communities working across and between grade level and content area teams to plan for personalization. In this way, PLE can become a long-term reality for learners' experiences in schools, rather than a short-term attempt at innovation in a single classroom or project.

Intrepid educators may consider all this and protest that "sometimes kids don't get to choose." And they'll be right, of course. There will always be times when we need to deliver direct instruction rather than setting learners free for self-directed discovery. And nothing about personalization negates the need for meeting knowledge-based curriculum standards; learners will still have common outcomes to achieve. But acknowledging these truths and working toward personalization are not at odds with each other. The more we learn about personalization as professionals, the more skilled and nuanced we can be in how we design learning and instruction. Gradually, we can build learning environments in which learners can experience ownership over their personal learning processes while still working toward the common goals.

THE NEED FOR A HOLISTIC APPROACH

At the risk of sounding redundant, it bears repeating, early and often, that PLE is not just one thing, nor is it defined by programs or tools. This matters greatly because there is a lot of room for schools to go wrong when they attempt to "do PLE" but oversimplify it in the process. It is absolutely appropriate for schools, or even individual educators, to start with small, structured steps and move along the continuum of PLE stages toward full implementation, and those steps may include getting comfortable with a new set of programs or tools. But plunking a program or tool into a teacher-centered classroom and declaring victory (or simply getting distracted by the myriad demands of working in public schools) will not change anything fundamental about whether learners are active or passive participants in their educational experiences. In that case, the program or tool will merely become part of the proverbial swinging pendulum. To achieve personalization, a more nuanced and holistic approach to putting the learner at the center is required.

All kinds of shifts may contribute toward implementing PLE, some of which have already been described in the Backpack section of this book. Replacing old-fashioned static furniture with more flexible learner workspaces (see chapter 3, "Learning Commons") can contribute to personalization by giving learners options to recognize how they work best and make decisions about what physical environments will help them be most productive for a given task. Structuring parts of the curriculum around inquiry (see chapter 4, "Inquiry-Based Learning") can give learners opportunities to thoughtfully choose the direction of their learning and connect the classroom content to their individual interests and passions. Coaching learners to develop a growth mindset (see chapter 5, "Growth Mindset and Grit") can facilitate strong connections between learner profiles, goal setting, and achieving success criteria as part of standards-based assessment practices. Establishing access to a makerspace (see chapter 6, "The Maker Movement") can dramatically increase the number of format options learners have available for multiple representations of their learning, both formal and informal.

In each of these cases, the Backpack item in isolation cannot make PLE happen. In fact, as discussed in each of those chapters, any Backpack item can fail to achieve its potential if oversimplified and shallowly implemented. But as part of a holistic approach, each has the potential to significantly contribute to learners' and educators' success at making the shift to personalization.

In general terms, the other set of tools most commonly thought to effect personalization is learner technology, particularly 1:1 device access. It is certainly true that it becomes far easier to offer learners choice and voice in how they pursue and show their learning in a 1:1 environment. That's partly because learners have plenty of access to online resources and digital creation apps, and partly because a modern learning management system gives educators much better tools to flexibly accept, track, and assess all those different learning options.

But digital technology use can become just as passive and teacher-centered as paper-and-pencil use if we don't back it up with a holistic commitment to letting learners drive decision-making. Assigning a learner to work through an online module at their own pace will free them from moving in lockstep with the rest of the class, but it won't give them an active role in deciding how they learn; the educator has still made all of the decisions about what happens in that module. Offering learners a choice between three digital format options for a project submission does not make learners into the constructors of their experiences if the educator has still made all the decisions to define those options. For technology in the classroom to fulfill its promise, educators must shift their roles away from teacher-centered approaches.

When we contemplate a shift as fundamental as changing who is in control of learning, it is easy to see how any educator or team might have the best of intentions but fall short of a successful implementation. This is why that pesky pendulum is always swinging; there is rarely time and space in public schools for educators to pause all of the other urgent demands on their attention and reimagine their practice. An individual absolutely can and should dabble and experiment and iterate in PLE, trying and trying again to see how personalized methods might look in their classrooms. But to truly cause long-term and widespread change, the commitment to PLE needs to come at the systems level. School leadership must commit to supporting educators in this profound change process, through resources, professional learning, and compassionate coaching so that they can grow their skills and confidence to release learning control without compromising learning quality and learner safety.

Personalized Learning in Explore

The Shared Foundation of Explore is rich with connections to personalized learning; indeed, once one starts looking at the Explore Competencies and Alignments with this lens, they appear to be everywhere! Learner choice, self-directed pursuits, resources, and strategies for inquiry-based processes—these elements that characterize Explore are marbled throughout the literature on personalization. As noted, the other Backpack chapters in this book can fold into various aspects of personalized learning practices, and so many of the connections found between those topics and Explore may also constitute PLE connections. For the purposes of this section, then, rather than trying to exhaust every possible way PLE may be found in this Shared Foundation, we'll zoom in on a few particularly salient areas.

DIGITAL LEARNING

Explore calls on school librarians to "[implement] technology as a tool or resource for learning" (AASL 2018, School Library V.B.1.), but it does not tell us how. This is entirely appropriate, especially over the length of time the AASL Standards are expected to endure, because technologies and technology-enabled practices change rapidly and depend heavily on the context in which learners and educators are operating. As mentioned earlier, of course, plunking technology in the middle of a teacher-centered classroom will not automatically cause it to become a learner-centered environment; the traditional context will far overpower the injection of 1:1 devices. Explore gives us tremendous room to make high-quality decisions about how to use the technology available to us, however, and those decisions can go a long way toward making the elements of PLE part of learners' and educators' everyday lives.

The professional knowledge required of school librarians to implement technology as a resource for learning is not dramatically different from that required to implement any other type of resource. This is welcome news for those of us who have in the past felt hesitant to step too far out into techie territory—it's not nearly as dangerous a ledge as we may fear! We select technologies using the same considerations we'd use for developing collections of print and audiovisual materials—which is to say, we think deeply about our users' needs, assess each resource's ability to meet those needs as well as its innate quality, make sure we collect a balance of resources available for both future and immediate needs, periodically remove resources that no longer meet needs, and deploy any instructional or promotional efforts necessary to ensure our users are able to effectively access and use the resources we've collected.

What likely feels different about selecting and implementing technology resources is a simple matter of gaining experience with the tools available. The way to solve that problem, too, is not dramatically different from how it is solved in other media: you get more experience by diving in and getting more experience. When a school librarian changes schools and finds themself serving a new grade band for which they don't know the literature, they gain experience by reading. They consult colleagues, awards lists, and so forth to determine which are the core titles everyone should know, and they watch their learners to determine what titles are currently popular, and they start reading those titles quickly and widely. For technology, the exact same steps can be followed: determine what the core tools are (probably a learning management system, a productivity suite, and perhaps a synchronous virtual learning platform); determine what else is currently popular for the target population, and start experimenting with prototypes quickly and widely.

Just as with traditional resource types, the way we implement technology most effectively for learning is through collaboration with other educators. This is particularly important when one of our purposes for implementing technology is to support a philosophical shift like that of personalizing learning. We can use our knowledge of what technology resources are available and how they work to support our educator partners' content knowledge and goals so that together we can collaboratively broaden and deepen everyone's pedagogical knowledge of how to create learner-centered experiences.

PERSONAL CURIOSITY

"Expressing curiosity about a topic of personal interest or curricular relevance" (AASL 2018, Learner and School Librarian V.C.1.) is so thoroughly baked into school libraries' DNA that it seems to defy explication, at least on the surface. What else are school libraries for, if not for supporting learners in acting on curiosity? When we look beyond that obvious and passionate raison d'etre and think more deliberately about the concrete ways school librarians actually perform that supportive work, an enormous vault of strategies emerges. A school librarian's skill at deploying those strategies purposefully and intentionally can make or break their success at creating a learner-centered environment that nurtures and cultivates personal interests.

For instance, let's look at the strategies involved in that most basic and core function of curiosity-feeding practice in school libraries: reading promotion. "Promoting reading" is not actually a single thing we do. Rather, reading promotion looks like a never-ending parade of strategies including book talks, book tastings, shelf talkers, genre studies, reading journals, book displays, book trailers, readers' advisory conferences—the list goes on. Some learners come naturally to reading, but others will need to be deliberately and repeatedly cultivated to it. Getting the right book at the right time in a learner's hands is a long-term and multifaceted process of tempting their curiosity about what a book contains, until that learner is sold that the contents will be worth the time invested in reading it. Once sold and satisfied, that learner may become the biggest advocate for that book in the future—but they may again require significant support to indulge curiosity about the next book. We take this long-term effort in stride as part of our core duties.

To create a personalized instructional environment in which learners are supported to become the drivers of their experiences, we (along with our collaborating educators) must extend this long-term, multifaceted work pattern to the way we encourage curiosity about learning. Strategies may include phenomena-based learning, in which we observe naturally occurring phenomena and ask personalized questions about them; "tasting" content by interacting with short texts on various subtopics and choosing which ones spark the most interest; designing tasks with authentic audiences so that learners have someone outside the classroom to impress with their work; or adapting any of the aforementioned reading promotion strategies to promote classroom content. Competitions are not recommended, however, for a simple reason: once one learner is made into a winner, the others are made into losers, and that is not conducive to curiosity and actively engaged learning.

Self-knowledge is among the most powerful strategies for supporting learners to act on curiosity in PLE. In the example of reading promotion, self-knowledge may look as simple as coaching a learner with questions like "what was the last book you really enjoyed?" or "what kinds of movies do you like to watch?" In a more comprehensive view of personalized learning, various kinds of self-knowledge (including answers to those readers' advisory questions and much more) can be gradually accrued in a learner profile. When learners understand their preferences, habits, tendencies, and competencies, they will be equipped in any new learning opportunity to search out the aspects of it that will appeal most to their curiosity.

COLLABORATIVE PROBLEM SOLVING

In Explore, both learners and school librarians are tasked with "collaboratively identifying innovative solutions to a challenge or problem" (AASL 2018, Learner and School Librarian V.C.3.). Both to understand this and to self-assess it in a school library, the easiest rule of thumb to consider is "who's doing the talking?" As school librarians, we often talk passionately and at length about the value of collaboration—but when we do so, we're usually referring to collaboration between ourselves and other educators. We don't always pay as much attention to collaboration between learners. But for learners to achieve this Competency in any meaningful way, we cannot leave it to chance. Collaboration is a sophisticated skill (that's why it has an entire Shared Foundation dedicated to it), and if we don't deliberately design it into learning experiences, much of learners' work will end up being fundamentally individual. If we look around a school library and realize that most of the discussion is between school librarians and learners, or that the conversations between learners are off-topic and therefore likely to be squashed, then we know that we've accidentally missed this Competency.

Why are we worried about collaborative problem solving in personalized learning? Remember, personalization is different from individualization. Though it's certainly a goal to break free from one-size-fits-all education, we're not trying to work toward an end in which no learner is ever working on the same thing or sharing cognitive space with another learner. Much to the contrary, one of the fundamental beliefs underpinning personalization is that knowledge is socially constructed. Creating opportunities for social construction through collaborative innovations and responses to challenges is among the most powerful ways PLE can be found in Explore.

When we ensure that our school library instruction and programming is designed to engender learner conversations first and foremost, what we're doing is addressing the most visible sign of putting decision-making in learners' hands. Each time we turn a conversation over to learners to collaborate among themselves around a worthwhile and interesting problem or challenge, we take a step closer to putting them at the center of their own learning experiences rather than keeping all the control in our hands. Because it is highly visible and therefore easy to monitor, maximizing learner collaboration can be an easy way to hold ourselves accountable to the goal of shifting our instructional roles toward coach and facilitator rather than central authority.

Carving out time and space for collaboratively responding to challenges during whole-class lessons, in makerspaces, in small-group rooms and other workspaces, and in other school library activities and environments allows for many of the elements of PLE to emerge. These collaborative conversations allow learners to make decisions based on their personal strengths and interests. They open up room to use a variety of resources, both high- and low-tech, that may be different from what other groups of learner collaborators are trying. They allow for multiple representations of learning to emerge, and they give license for school librarians and other educators to assess learning by how well those representations show mastery of the standards rather than how well individuals complied with an teacher-driven task.

FEEDBACK FOR GROWTH

Explore's final Competency in the *AASL Standards Framework for Learners,* which asks learners to "open-mindedly [accept] feedback for positive and constructive growth" (AASL 2018, Learner and School Librarian V.D.3.), is one that school librarians often endorse but may not be sure how to actualize. Because so many of us come from traditional school environments (both as professionals and as student learners), it can be easy for us to think of open-mindedness and willingness to accept feedback as character traits that are inborn or that spontaneously appear in blessed individuals. That may certainly be true for a few individuals. But according to Carol Dweck's research (see chapter 5), mindset matters a great deal in developing qualities like these, and these traits can be learned like any other skill. Our task, as described in the School Librarian parallel for this Learner Competency, is to foster an atmosphere in which that learning can happen.

By putting learners at the center and reframing school librarians' instructional roles as coach and facilitator, PLE is an excellent construct for fostering this atmosphere. When we lean into the precepts of personalization, we are working within a model of practice that prioritizes helping learners make their own high-quality decisions to drive their learning. And a major way we can do that is by providing high-quality feedback.

School librarians sometimes struggle with the role feedback should play in our instruction because we're often operating in very different instructional conditions than other educators. If we're teaching on a flexible schedule, we may not have much time with a group of learners before they return to classrooms to finish their projects, which makes summative feedback difficult because we may not ever see the end results of learners' work. And if we're teaching on a fixed schedule, we are likely responsible for seeing our entire school on a weekly basis, which makes giving detailed feedback to all learners a daunting prospect.

PLE offers several ways of thinking about how to bring together and relieve some of these issues. It emphasizes assessment *as* learning and *for* learning rather than assessment *of* learning—which is to say, it integrates assessment and feedback to inform learner's work throughout the learning process, rather than postponing feedback until it becomes an all-or-nothing process. This is a much better match for school librarians' unique schedules. Standards-based assessment practices measure mastery of learning targets rather than averaging a barrage of assignment scores. This frees school librarians to have feedback conversations with learners about the quality of their work, as opposed to investing time and energy in the type of numerical grades that many in our profession find problematic. Structures like learner profiles and collaborative conversation protocols can engage learners in tracking their own progress and giving feedback to each other, which relieves the school librarian from being solely responsible for feedback to a large number of learners.

Collaborative planning, as with many parts of school library practice, is key for realizing our vision for a high-quality feedback cycle. Working tightly with educator partners to define how learning will be coached, when, and by whom is the best way to ensure that we're fostering an atmosphere in which learners expect and open-mindedly accept that feedback. When feedback is given in connection with a collaboratively planned and intrinsically motivating task that is well-designed for actively engaged learning and driven by the principles of personalization, it becomes powerful fuel for learner-driven positive growth for all members of the school community.

Personalized Learning: Implementation Examples and Analysis

Everyday implementation of the principles of personalization and the Explore Competencies and Alignments to which they're tightly connected can take a wide variety of forms in the school library. Following are several implementation examples, with each pair contrasting more and less effective executions of a similar idea, in the context of Explore's four Domains. The accompanying analysis notes are designed to help you understand what makes one example of practice stronger than another so that you'll be able to reflect on how their elements compare to your own practice and make decisions about some areas for professional growth you might like to pursue.

DOMAIN: THINK

Scenario: You want your learners to fully explore and broaden their reading tastes.

Example A	Example B
• Host a schoolwide genre challenge. • Create a menu of different genres with a Top Ten list of books and authors in each, and promote it to learners in all classes. • Post the menu on bulletin boards along with cover art of the featured books and post online with the books' video trailers. • Get other educators involved by making signs for their classroom and office doors showing what they're currently reading. • Seek community partners to donate fabulous prizes to the learners who complete the challenge by finishing three books in every genre by the end of the year.	• Teach learners to create reading journals to log what they've enjoyed and why. • Create a variety of promotional resources, such as rotating bulletin boards with cover art, book trailers, and Top Ten lists for a variety of books and authors in various genres. • Allow learners to explore these resources regularly to find ideas of what they'd like to try next, and encourage them to step out of their comfort zones. • In their reading journals, they should record what they perused, what they chose, and how it went. • Not liking or finishing a book is okay! • Coach learners to reflect in their journals about what each book attempt taught them about their taste.

Although both of these examples represent similar intended outcomes, Example A is centered on the efforts of the school librarian to broaden learners' reading, while Example B supports learners at the center of their own reading journeys. Example A gives learners some choices, but they are all options dictated by the school librarian creating the genre menu. Example B includes some of the same promotional efforts, though fewer flashy attention-grabbers; however, it is organized in such a way that all of the motivation is intrinsic and actions result from learners' decision-making.

DOMAIN: CREATE

Scenario: You're interested in how flexible seating might help learners become more focused and productive.

Example A	Example B
• After noticing a pattern in their learner profiles that many learners have developed self-knowledge about their need to wiggle during class instead of sitting too long, do some research about how other educators address this problem. • Select a few exemplar options from blogs and open a brainstorming conversation with learners. If funding were available, what environment would best suit them? • Based on their feedback, use grant funding to buy a couple of bean bags and exercise balls. • Have a class discussion about what seating options might be best for different types of tasks. When learners try each, ask them to reflect on how the type of seating affected their experience. • If a positive trend emerges, or if neither option was successful, seek another grant to purchase more seating or try different options based on learners' experiences.	• After seeing a lot of exciting discussion in blogs and reading reviews about how updated environments benefit learners, use grant money to purchase enough sets of wobbly stools, bike desks, bean bags, and exercise balls to replace most of the tables and chairs in the school library. • Host a big ribbon-cutting party to generate excitement about the school library's new look. • Because there aren't quite enough of the new seating options for everyone in a full class to use, another grant will be needed. • Devise a system to keep track of who sat in which new zone so that learners can be rotated through the options on each class visit and everyone will get a fair turn at everything.

Both of these examples attempt to provide more flexibility in the learning environment, but only Example A takes a learner-centered approach. In Example A, the school librarian seeks and uses funding based on learners' self-knowledge that has emerged through PLE instructional strategies, with learners as co-creators of their experiences even when the school librarian necessarily has to be the sole grant-seeker on their behalf. In Example B, the school librarian's actions and intentions are all based on the input of other educators, and learners do not get to drive their own use of the new environment.

DOMAIN: SHARE

Scenario: Your school wants to start offering learners some choice and voice in how they learn, so you volunteer to help with a pilot project.

Example A	Example B
• In collaboration with a classroom educator, develop an inquiry unit in which learners can choose their own research topics. • Work together with the educator to analyze the curriculum and determine a variety of possible topics that will meet the standards and can be well-supported by high-quality resources available in the school library. • On learners' first day of research, allow them to browse the resources available for each topic before selecting their preference from the list.	• In collaboration with classroom educators, develop a basic protocol that learners can use to select their own topics for research and inquiry. • The protocol includes steps for learners like monitoring their progress on previous assessments so they'll know what standards they still need to master, identifying areas of interest based on their learner profiles, browsing the school library's resources to see what is available, and then synthesizing all of these sources to select an inquiry focus. • Use this protocol with learners each time an inquiry unit is planned so that they practice and internalize these skills over time.

Example A gives learners quite a few choices for their learning, and all of them are vetted to ensure that they will support learners' success. However, all of these choices have been defined by the school librarian and classroom educator. Example B expects more cognitive work from learners, and it introduces the risk that learners may not make terrific choices. However, it allows learners to engage in driving their own decisions, and over time mitigates the risk by helping them practice and grow their decision-making ability, which is more in line with PLE. In Example A, the school librarian's time and effort will be spent vetting topics and resources before learners arrive; in Example B, the school librarian will spend that time and energy coaching learners as they work through the protocol.

DOMAIN: GROW

Scenario: The school wants every educator in the building to concentrate on assessing student learning.

Example A	Example B
• The school librarian focuses on making sure that every kind of activity that may take place in the school library has a metric attached. • During every lesson or programming session learners are given an exit ticket, which the school librarian collects and grades on paper for the youngest learners. • Older learners are taught to complete their exit tickets using online forms or quizzes in the learning management system so that the grading is a little faster. • When collaborating with classroom educators, the school librarian requests copies of all learner project submissions so that the librarian can give detailed comments as feedback. • When learners access the makerspace, the school librarian photographs each thing they make as evidence of what is being produced and categorizes these photos as Emerging, Proficient, or Achieving.	• In the early part of the school year, during orientation and basic procedural instruction, the school librarian invests some time in showing learners Emerging, Proficient, and Achieving exemplars of several types of activities they might expect to engage in in the school library. • Based on the evidence they observe in these exemplars of what constitutes the different quality levels of performance, learners contribute input toward the development of success criteria for library learning. • After collecting input from learners, the school librarian organizes these success criteria in a rubric and teaches learners to use this rubric to self-assess their work in the school library. • During units, there is time planned for learners to use the rubric to give each other feedback and to use that feedback to improve their own work. • The school librarian references the rubric when coaching learners on improving their work.

Both of these examples show creativity on the part of the school librarian when trying to respond to a school initiative that is not a perfect fit to their traditionally ungraded workflow. Example A represents a tremendous effort without much bang for the buck, however, with the school librarian producing large amounts of data that does not affect learners' next steps (assuming they even receive it). Example B, in contrast, requires a time investment early in the year to co-create success criteria, but then moves most of the effort onto learners. This approach is more appropriate for learner-centered PLE; it puts the feedback process in learners' hands so they can drive it, and it streamlines the school librarian's workflow. It also offers a better chance to help learners master the Explore Competency of accepting feedback for positive growth, because co-creation, self-assessment, and facilitation ensure that learners have a clear vision of where they are versus where they need to be.

COMPASS CHECK

Questions for the Reflective Practitioner

1. What are some examples of teacher-centered and learner-centered practices in your current school library operations? What about in other places in your school?
2. Think about your own experiences as a learner. How might those experiences have been different if the principles of personalization had been applied? What might change for today's learners?
3. What might be some short-term and long-term steps to take that could help move your school library toward the next stage of PLE?

PART III

Boots

In the age of information overload, decision fatigue is often our mortal enemy. With a full spectrum of big ideas and tiny details bombarding us from every direction, forcing us to evaluate and weigh and judge and sort, our brains just get tired of dealing with the onslaught. Decision fatigue results in all kinds of choices we might not make if our brains weren't so tired. This may be why we grab junk food at the cashier station after we've considered which of a huge number of items we might want for dinner as we worked our way through a supermarket, impulsively buy expensive clothing after we've tried to choose more reasonably priced items from a tower of outfits that didn't fit, or agreed to purchase a dubious and expensive auto maintenance plan after we've painstakingly weighed which model to buy before committing to a new car. It can even be why we yell at our kids, after we've expended all our energy making professional decisions during a long day at work.

In addition to prompting bad behaviors, decision fatigue can cause us to decide not to act, in order to mitigate the risk of a wrong move. This is very important in the context of professional learning because it means simple decision fatigue can make it extremely difficult to implement the variety of new ideas and methods we've encountered. As educators, school librarians make hundreds or even thousands of decisions every day. We get completely stuck in our old practices—not because we are scared of or resistant to change, but because in our information-overloaded environments, our brains are simply too tired to make the choices involved in trying a new way.

The Boots section of this book is designed to get you moving with the new ideas you're exploring. It doesn't do us much good to have our Backpacks full and our Compass pointed at the horizon if our feet get stuck in a patch of quicksand or bitten by a snake, bringing our whole journey to a halt! Boots protect our feet from the unexpected when we move through new terrain, so that even in tough swampy territory, we can continue making the decisions necessary to move safely ahead, one step at a time.

Similarly, the activities in this section will help you protect your learning and your intentions to move in new directions of practice, even on tough and unpredictable days at work. Developing a detailed strategic plan with iterative rounds of stakeholder feedback will help you work methodically through the huge decision-making load required to implement new techniques, so that decision fatigue is less likely to pop up during your implementation and prevent you from moving forward. By bringing Boots to the Shared Foundation of Explore, you'll be equipped to put one foot in front of the other in service of traveling toward your desired destination or setting out on new journeys.

8

From New Learning to Action

When I introduce the AASL Standards to groups of school librarians, administrator partners, or other educators, one of the first things I point out is that there are Domains and Competencies for *learners,* not for *students*. This was a deliberate choice on the part of the AASL Standards editorial board because it acknowledges that everyone who interacts with the school library may be acting in the role of learner at various times. Certainly, our students are learners on a daily basis, but also our classroom educators, administrators, parents, and other members of our school communities may be functioning as learners at different times and on different topics. That role can even fluctuate within a single conversation. For instance, during a collaborative planning conversation, a school librarian might mention a resource or tool that a classroom educator is not familiar with; that educator's role will briefly flex into learner mode while the school librarian helps them understand this new information and construct new knowledge, and then return to their role as an expert to decide how to integrate this tool into instructional plans.

This role-flexing most certainly applies to us as school librarians. As instructional leaders, it is incumbent upon us that for our students to become lifelong learners, we must go first by modeling lifelong learning. When we are intentional and transparent about what it looks and feels like to be a learner, then the other members of our school communities can feel comfortable coming along for the journey. It can be scary and uncomfortable to be a learner! Choosing to learn is a vulnerable thing, because it requires admitting to ourselves and others that we have areas where we don't yet know everything. However, it is also one of the greatest joys of life to learn and expand our horizons. How fortunate we are to work in a field that values learning and puts it at the center of our professional practice!

The Backpack section of this book discusses a number of important concepts and frameworks for deepening and enriching our school library practice. Working through these ideas can show us exactly what flexing into the role of learner might look like for a school librarian. However, that comes with a caveat: to behave as a learner involves not just reading about important ideas, but truly working and "chewing" on them. It requires that we make the deliberate choice to be vulnerable about our practice, search through ideas to discover what we have not yet mastered in our practice, and find new things we would like to try in real life to improve, or even transform, ourselves in the context of our school libraries. Especially if we are ambitious, it may even require that we fail or fall short on our first efforts, then go back and try again—"iteratively responding to challenges" (AASL 2018, Learner V.D.1.), just as we expect our student learners to do.

Explore as Professional Development

The Boots section of this book is designed to support your thought process as a learner as you "discover and innovate in a growth mindset developed through experience and reflection" (AASL 2018, 104). I love that phrase! This Key Commitment for Explore is as good a description as I've ever heard of what excellent professional development ought to be! Discovery and innovation are exactly what will push our practice forward throughout our careers, no matter the specific needs of our schools. Experience and reflection are what will allow us to do this, gradually and continuously, getting a little better every single day. And growth mindset is what will make us feel inspired and motivated to keep growing and improving, even when we're already doing terrific work, so that our practice is not only good for our schools but also good for our souls.

However, let's be real—how often do we attend professional development (PD) sessions and leave feeling like they were good for our soul? Too often, we instead leave feeling drained, discouraged, or frustrated. Sometimes this is because the sessions are being offered after school, when we are tired from working a long day before we even get there and it is just plain difficult to summon soul-sustaining energy in that worn-out state. In many districts, the problem may be poor tailoring; it can be very difficult to find local PD options that are aimed at librarians, and the available topics may require quite a bit of translation to feel relevant to our work. Sometimes, as with a conference or large-scale training, the event as a whole may leave us feeling terrific in the moment even though we can't point to any specific session or part of the PD that was well matched to our needs. That usually means that the positivity we've experienced is about the social benefits of getting together with other members of our tribe, rather than about anything in particular we've learned, and so those terrific feelings may not last when we return home.

The reality is that most traditional PD is not particularly well designed for our needs when we are in learner mode. Traditional PD presentations, even when they are on interesting topics and delivered by entertaining speakers, are predicated on the idea that we will sit quietly, listen to what someone else has done, then go back to work, and, in our spare time, figure out how to implement this in our own practice. But even if we did not have thorough research and documentation that lecture is an ineffective format for learning—which we do—this is a model that is destined to fail almost every time. For educators, spare time at work simply does not exist! Our professional learning cannot depend on the premise that we will listen passively and then figure it out later, when later will probably never come. Instead, our real work as professional learners comes in much the same way it comes for our student learners: when we are actively involved in exploring ideas.

Snapshot of Practice: What Explore-as-Professional Development Might Look Like

There are as many options for and ways of thinking about professional learning as there are for student learning. Indeed, when we ourselves are the learners, it's possible there are exponentially more! For our student learners, there is guidance from research, state and national content standards, and time-honored wisdom that we can use to determine what are the most important things for young people to know and master. But for us, once we leave graduate school, we often feel we are navigating uncharted waters when confronting what comes next. We might have school or district priorities to guide us, but just as often we might feel that the proverbial swinging pendulum in education renders some of those initiatives difficult to invest our time and energy in. Even in ideal working conditions, the online community gives us something of an unlimited cornucopia of terrific ideas to consider pursuing in our practice. Where does one begin to learn?

In my district, as in other districts around the country, that question really does not have a single right answer. Even though we're a large enough district to have a school library supervisor to lead some centralized guidance about school library vision and priorities, we still have ninety school sites that each have different needs and priorities, which means that each of our school librarians has a different set of learning needs. So in my district, we do not try to define, in any universal way, the right things to learn or the right way to learn them. Instead, for several years now we've been experimenting with a form of personalized professional development that, with the advent of the *National School Library Standards*, turns out to be well-aligned with the Shared Foundation of Explore.

What does that look like for us?[1] School librarians in our district by and large no longer attend "sit and get" presentations. Instead, they have a variety of workshop and discussion formats to choose from, all of which are centered around a learning and implementation focus (LIF) plan for the year—a structured way of thinking about and problem solving for the real problems of practice they're facing in their buildings. The LIF planning process is modeled on principles from inquiry-based and personalized learning theories (see chapters 4 and 7) and is designed to create a common structure to walk school librarians through the messy and complicated work of identifying their professional learning needs and creating a plan for how to pursue them, even when no one else around them may be working on the same issues. Workshops are predicated on the idea that each school librarian will start by self-assessing to identify a real need for growth in their practice, and then a series of discussion structures and protocols will help them think through where they are, where they want to be, and how they'll get there. Participants use a workbook to help them record their thinking and their progress. PD sessions are all about convening groups of their colleagues to give each other support and feedback along the way.

What might that look like for school librarians in other districts, especially those who may have fewer PD resources available to them? Happily, there is no need for a formal workshop to begin this kind of thinking and learning. The Boots Planning Guide in chapter 9 (a version of the LIF workbook my own district uses) will provide you with much of the structure you'll need to walk through your own messy, creative, Explore-as-PD journey. The particular advantages of a workshop—dedicated time set aside for difficult thinking and a group of like-minded peers to discuss and share with along the way—are things that can be planned for in any setting, as you design a solution that's right for your local situation and needs.

When thinking through the logistics of planning for our own professional learning, it's important to remember the signature truism of working in education: most people tend to teach the way they were taught. If we want to teach or practice in new and exciting ways, or if we are responsible for leading others to do so, it is crucial that we look for opportunities to be taught in those ways. Participating in PD that takes place primarily through exploration of ideas, personalized inquiry, and solving real-life problems of practice will help school librarians experience these principles as learners. Working through Explore in the learner mode will make us better equipped to implement these Standards with our own student learners.

How to Use the Explore Planning Guide

The Planning Guide in the next chapter is designed to help you experience professional development through the lens of Explore, regardless of what types of PD are available locally for you. As you work through it, you are likely to recognize some direct connections between its elements and the Learner Competencies outlined in Explore, such as:

- Reflecting and questioning assumptions and possible misconceptions (AASL 2018, Learner V.A.2.)
- Problem solving through cycles of design, implementation, and reflection (AASL 2018, Learner V.B.1.)

- Persisting through self-directed pursuits by tinkering and making (AASL 2018, Learner V.B.2.)
- Collaboratively identifying innovative solutions to a challenge or problem (AASL 2018, Learner V.C.3.)
- Iteratively responding to challenges (AASL 2018, Learner V.D.1.)
- Open-mindedly accepting feedback for positive and constructive growth (AASL 2018, Learner V.D.3.)

The Planning Guide itself does not provide new information for you to learn from. Rather, because professional learning can be an exceptionally messy, open-ended, and often bewildering process, the Planning Guide offers a structure to support you when reflecting on your practice and making thoughtful decisions about what you want to work on and how you can best work on it. The abundant information available to you through books and articles, other trainings you may have attended, materials provided by your district, social media, or other sources can all then be folded into your plan as needed. You are of course welcome to work through the Planning Guide using ideas you encountered in the Backpack section of this book, or you may prefer to loop in another exciting idea or topic you've encountered that is matched to your immediate needs. Innovating by combining multiple concepts is always welcome and appropriate if you feel confident in tackling it that way.

These five additional pieces of advice may help you in working through this process successfully:

1. **While the Planning Guide is flexible and can be adapted for unique professional learning situations, it is probably best to follow it fairly closely, especially on the first try.** That's simply because the type of thinking it describes is difficult, much more so than traditional passive PD experiences, and it requires participants to accept the temporary discomfort of wading through ambiguity. Most learners will have a more productive experience working through that type of thinking if they rely on the structure to support them (just as inquiry frameworks support student learning, as described in chapter 4).
2. **Try to enlist at least one colleague to work through the process alongside you.** They don't have to be working on the same project as you, just using the same structure. Groups of three to five participants are ideal, if possible. Your partners will be invaluable for generating ideas when you are stuck and providing feedback to help you refine your thinking. Possible partners might be found among other school librarians in your district, members of your local AASL Chapter organization, collaborating educators in your building, or even administrators or community partners who are interested in enriching the work of your school library.

3. **Schedule a dedicated time and place to do this work.** If thinking through how to tackle difficult problems of practice was easy, we'd already be doing it all the time! Because it is not easy work, it will be tempting to let it slide behind the other time-pressured craziness of everyday life in a busy school library. Set yourself up for success by deciding (with your partners, as applicable) when you'll best be able to dedicate time, attention, and energy for this work. Think through what environment (home, school, coffee shop, virtual, etc.) will be best for you, too. Then put it on the calendar and stick to it!
4. **Resist the temptation to leave your learning on paper!** Remember that the Planning Guide is just that: a guide for planning. But what you're planning for is what you intend to *do*. Every step of this process is meant to be implemented in your practice. Implementation is the only way you'll know whether the ideas you captured in the Planning Guide are working. So as you explore new ideas and think through tough problems, make sure to try them out!
5. **Be ready to iterate.** The process of exploring as professional learning is iterative in nature. Feel free to use the Planning Guide for a major project, or to work through it multiple times for several small projects. Along the way, whether you're checking in during a long arc or completing a short one, you are always free to make adjustments, incorporate new information, or go back and try something again with a different tactic. Making changes isn't cheating or displaying weakness—it is exactly what Explore asks effective learners to do.

At all points in your professional learning journey, as you explore new and exciting ways to innovate and grow your practice, remember to give yourself grace at those times when the work feels challenging. There are no easy answers—if there were one right way to solve the problems of a school library, then somebody smart would have already figured it out and told everybody! Laboring our way through difficult, ambiguous problems, often complicated by the many restrictions inherent in our school-community environments, is exactly what makes us professionals. Learning is some of the most important work we can do. And it is worth leaning into the struggle, in order to create better outcomes for all the learners we lead.

NOTE

1. For readers who may be curious for a little more detail about how professional development for school librarians is approached in my district, see my *Knowledge Quest* article (Searles 2019).

9

Your Explore Planning Guide

It's time to put those proverbial boots on the ground and start exploring! As professional learners, we're committed to "discover and innovate in a growth mindset developed through experience and reflection" (AASL 2018, 104). This Planning Guide is a structure designed to support you in doing that, through the completion of six activities:

- Activity 1: Self-Assessment
- Activity 2: Focus Definition
- Activity 3: Action Steps
- Activity 4: Problems and Solutions
- Activity 5: Project Mapping
- Activity 6: Summative Feedback

Each of these activities is designed to guide your thinking, through the type of learning that is described in the Explore Competencies. Every activity description corresponds to an activity worksheet at the end of this chapter (see pages 130–137), which you will use for recording and organizing your work. You can engage in these activities as an individual or you can recruit a group of colleagues to work on it as a group. For those who might want to organize these activities into a formal workshop series, see Appendix B for some helpful hints.

As a professional learning process, this structure will serve you regardless of the particulars of what you're learning about right now. The Planning Guide can be applied to any content you want to work with, and you do not need to choose that content before you begin. In fact, I strongly advise you *not* to choose that content before you've had a chance to complete the self-assessment and focus-definition activities, because those are designed to help you think critically about what kind of content you really want to focus on based on your needs! This structure is iterative, and you can Explore with it as many times as you'd like; you can circle back to any part of the process at any point during your learning cycle, or you can work through it to completion and then start afresh with new needs and goals in mind.

By the end of this process, you'll have created a thoughtful, detailed, and practical plan to achieve and implement one or more ambitious new ideas in your practice as a school librarian. You'll know you have been successful if your plan is:

- **Innovative**—Your plan should represent work that is new, both to you and to the people you serve.
- **Specific**—Your plan should include making decisions about the who, what, when, where, why, and how of what you want to achieve.
- **Actionable**—Your plan should be based on factors you can control or influence in your real life, not "if only" conditional wishes.
- **Needs-Based**—Your plan should be driven by the unique needs of the community you serve, in that community's current conditions.

As you work, be ambitious and brave. It is a good and joyful thing to venture into unfamiliar territory—that is how our worlds become bigger! If we were always to remain in tried-and-true areas in which we already felt confident, then we wouldn't be discovering and innovating. The right answers may not even exist yet for the problems you're working on, but this professional learning structure is a vehicle to help you seek them. So be a courageous explorer as you prepare to Think, Create, Share, and Grow your practice.

Activity 1: Self-Assessment

GETTING ORGANIZED	
Intended outcome:	Clarify strengths and areas for refinement in your school library practice in order to choose a well-aligned focus for professional growth.
You'll need...	• Worksheet for Activity 1: Self-Assessment on page **130** • Optional: scratch paper
Approximate time commitment:	• About 15–20 minutes if working individually • About 30–45 minutes if discussing with a group
Next steps...	• May move on to Activity 2 immediately if desired

When you tackle ambitious new learning, you're essentially leading a change effort. That might be small-scale, as when you're learning to shift something about your personal habits and practices, or on a larger -scale, as when you're learning to implement a whole-school project that involves numerous stakeholders, or anywhere in between. To lead this change effectively, it is helpful to begin with the destination in mind. So you will start by establishing your desired outcomes, not only of this as-yet-undefined project but of your work in general: What do you want to see as the fruits of your professional labor?

First, you'll consider this question through three different stakeholder lenses:

- **Learners:** What are the qualities we want learners to have when they leave our programs?
- **Educators:** What are the qualities we want other educators to develop as a result of working with us?
- **School community:** When parents and other community members talk to their friends, what do we want them to say about how our school libraries affect their children?

Prioritize your top two or three desired outcomes for each of these audiences. If you're working in a group, you may benefit from discussing your ideas aloud to explore and refine them before writing them down. If you're working individually, you may find it helpful to begin with an open-ended "quick write" on scratch paper, then give yourself a little processing time before moving your polished thoughts over to the worksheet. Either way, once you've narrowed and recorded your desired outcomes, this will give you a concise list of priorities for what you hope to achieve in the big picture.

Next, you'll narrow that big-picture viewpoint by considering four different categories of outputs related to your work.

- **Productive and Social Relationships:** This may include any and all of the people your school library serves. School librarians need both productive and social relationships in order to thrive in their practice; sometimes, one type can lead to the other.
- **Environment and Infrastructure:** This category comprises all the stuff your school library uses to serve its community—your collection, physical environment, tools and technology, procedures, and so forth.
- **Stakeholder Perceptions of the School Library:** This category encompasses what each of your stakeholders perceive about your work: what feedback (forthright or subtle) do you receive that gives you clues about what other people truly think and feel about your school library?
- **Core Values in School Librarianship:** This category asks you to think back to your graduate education when you studied to become a school librarian. How are you doing at keeping your "real life" connected to the ideals and the most important work of school librarianship?

Succinctly describe what you believe these outputs currently look like in your practice. For instance, for Environment and Infrastructure, you might make notes that look like this:

> Collection is getting there, did a ton of weeding last year, still need to find more books for my ELL population. People aren't really using the digital materials yet, even though we've got good stuff; must be a knowledge gap somewhere. Bought makerspace stuff with the grant last summer, still gotta figure out how to advertise it.

Finally, continue narrowing your big ideas toward action by quantitatively self-assessing how you're doing in each of the stakeholder lenses and work categories. For each of them, assign yourself a percentage score. For instance, based on the notes above, perhaps you feel like your Environment and Infrastructure is at about 60 percent of the level you'd like it to be. This will help you clearly see and understand your current practice, as well as untangling your outputs from your desired outcomes. Breaking down your self-assessment into several different analytical views, both qualitative and quantitative, will help you gain clarity on what specific elements may be particular strengths or areas for refinement before you start to choose a path forward.

Activity 2: Focus Definition

GETTING ORGANIZED	
Intended outcome:	Define a narrow focus for professional learning that will help you build on your strengths and grow in your areas for refinement.
You'll need...	• Worksheet for Activity 2: Focus Definition on page **131** • Optional: colored pens or other preferred sketching tools
Approximate time commitment:	• About 25–30 minutes if working individually • About 30–45 minutes if discussing with a group
Next steps...	• If possible, set work aside for "marination time" (overnight or up to a week) before moving on to Activity 3.

Now that you've self-assessed where you want to be and where you are right now through several different lenses, you'll start synthesizing those elements together into a desired pathway for professional learning. Look back at the notes you've taken so far: what jumps out at you? What pieces of your self-assessment give you a strong or emotional reaction? What connections or mismatches do you see between your desired outcomes and your percentage self-scores?

Start by illustrating your strengths, growth areas, and their intersections visually. Use as few words as possible, sketching concepts whenever you can. Arrows, circles, and other graphical elements are helpful to group or divide ideas, order them, and show relationships among them. Stick figures and other cartoonish elements are allowed and encouraged if they help you represent your ideas. If you are working in a group, share your drawings. The process of explaining your visual representation to others will help you refine and clarify your thinking, so if you realize something new or change your mind as you share, change it on your drawing—that was a growth opportunity, not a mistake!

After beginning to synthesize your thoughts visually, you will start to see your problem of practice emerging, though it likely feels rather cloudy. The next step is to start adding a few details to cut through that cloudiness and increase its clarity by making it more fleshed-out and concrete. Record your targeted, concise notes on your most current thinking in each of these three categories:

- **High priority needs:** Of all the needs of your school community right now, which are the highest priority? What will make the biggest difference or remove the toughest barriers for the people you serve?
- **High leverage learning:** What might be the crucial knowledge, skills, practices, or approaches you can gain that would help you target those needs? What skill set would help you get at the root cause of the issue, rather than only the symptoms?
- **Personal strengths:** What are some current practices and experiences you can lean on as you address those high-priority needs? Which of your innate tendencies and character traits will support you to overcome challenges?

Converting your visual thoughts back into words may feel redundant, but it also may feel like an uncomfortable shift. If you find yourself feeling mentally "sandpapered," celebrate that temporary discomfort, because that's what learning feels like!

Finally, clarify your intent by drafting a narrow Focus Statement clearly stating what you want to do as a result of your professional learning work. Creating this statement is important, because if you can't clearly communicate your focus in only a few words, then your intent really isn't focused yet. And if it isn't focused yet, then you aren't going to be effective at turning it into an actionable plan. A solid and cogent Focus Statement, however, will give you a concrete view of exactly what you want to achieve so that you'll be able to effectively devise plans for achieving it.

If you are working in a group, share your statements with each other. Offer feedback on each other's statements if you want, or just let them alone for now, depending on the group's comfort level. Then, I recommend putting the statement away for some marination time—preferably overnight, or perhaps even a week—before moving on to the next stages of your work. Rest assured that you can still adjust it later if needed! Your brain will continue processing your Focus Statement in the background so that your thinking will be clearer and more effective when you return to it for the next steps.

Activity 3: Action Steps

GETTING ORGANIZED	
Intended outcome:	Generate ideas for growth and implementation actions that will provide opportunities for professional learning in alignment with your Focus Statement.
You'll need...	• Worksheet for Activity 3: Action Steps on page **133** • Timer • Optional: scratch paper
Approximate time commitment:	• About 15–25 minutes if working individually • About 45–60 minutes if discussing with a group
Next steps...	• May move on to Activity 4 immediately if desired • If convenient, taking a short marination time (e.g., a lunch break) before Activity 4 is appropriate.

This next activity is perhaps the most familiar part of the process: simple, open-ended brainstorming of possible action steps. You'll write down the current version of your Focus Statement, describe your target audience for the change you're hoping to make, and start to generate possible action steps for your journey of exploration-as-professional-learning.

If your Focus Statement is unchanged since creating it in the last activity, after the marination time you were hopefully able to take, then just write down the same thing again. However, if you've since had ideas to revise or refine your statement after placing it on the backburner for a little time (and many people will!), then put in your newest version. As you work through the remainder of this Planning Guide, continue using your newest version each time an activity calls for your Focus Statement. Resist the temptation to feel guilty or doubtful about altering your statement at any point in the process! Changing your mind is a good and joyful thing, because it means you are refining your ideas and making them better. Iterating is far preferable to sticking with an early idea that isn't a good fit. Regularly improving and clarifying your focus will result in much better outcomes for your learners than holding onto an old idea out of sheer stubbornness.

Describing your target audience does not need to be lengthy or laborious. However, it is worth specifying in writing exactly who you hope will be helped, supported, shifted, or otherwise impacted by the professional learning you are undertaking. All work in school libraries is ultimately meant to impact people, so we do our best work when we're keeping those people at the forefront of our action design. This description will be most helpful to you if you can be as specific and narrow as possible because pinpointing exactly who is in your audience will tell you more about their needs and better help you decide where your explorations should take you in the course of what you're learning and attempting. Thus, although "my learners" would be a typical audience that we're always trying to serve, "my upper elementary learners" sheds much more light on the audience's probable needs, and "my fourth and fifth grade learners who will be transitioning soon to middle school, as well as their parents and educators" is clearer still. The latter provides a better path for making decisions about what new professional learning you may want to explore to strengthen your practice.

When you brainstorm action steps, you'll want to generate as many possibilities for yourself as possible. The longer your list, the better—grab scratch paper and fill multiple pages if you can! Set a timer for ten minutes and write down as many ideas as you can think of. Try not to let your pencil stop moving! As you do this, it's important that you keep a mindset of possibility, rather than one of limitation. So when you write down ideas, don't stop to judge or evaluate them, or to think about whether they are even possible for you. Just write them down and rest assured that you can pass judgment later. If you get stuck at any point during the ten minutes, start writing down ideas that *will not* work. Writing down bad ideas on purpose will decrease your stress about getting everything right, and is highly likely to unlock your imagination and get the good ideas flowing again soon thereafter.

If you're working in a group, generate your ideas aloud. Set aside ten minutes for each participant (this is most manageable in groups of three or four) and talk about one person's Focus Statement at a time so that everyone has a chance to benefit from the wide-ranged thinking of the group.

Afterward, go back to your high-quantity list of possible action steps and start pruning it down to high-quality ideas. Look at everything that was generated: are there any similar ideas that can be synthesized or consolidated? Are there any unrealistic ideas that can be improved to become something truly actionable? Are there any vague or broad ideas that can be clarified into something (or multiple somethings) more specific by adding details? Are there weak ideas you can turn into stronger ones, or ideas that simply need to be weeded off the list? After looking back at the earlier list, do you have entirely new and better ideas that you'd like to replace some of the old ones? Once you've improved and narrowed the action steps on your list, you're ready to start moving closer to action.

Activity 4: Problems and Solutions

GETTING ORGANIZED	
Intended outcome:	Anticipate possible barriers to success of planned action steps and seek help refining plans to lower those barriers.
You'll need...	• Worksheet for Activity 4: Problems and Solutions on page **134** • Timer • Colleagues to serve as thought partners
Approximate time commitment:	• About 7–10 minutes for individual work, plus an additional 3 minutes per thought partner • If thought partners are not gathered in a single group, this activity can be spread out over several days in order to meet each thought partner individually, if needed.
Next steps...	• If possible, set aside some marination time (overnight if possible) before moving on to Activity 5.

At this point in your journey, having assembled a list of top-notch possibilities for high-quality action steps, it's highly likely that you have some "yeah, but..." thoughts about implementing those steps. That's a completely natural reaction when you are exploring types of professional work you've never attempted before—remember, learning is inherently messy and vulnerable. In fact, if you don't have any doubts about your ability to readily accomplish the things on your list, then the list is probably not ambitious enough! If that's the case, then you may want to return to either your Focus Statement or your Action Steps activity and look for places where you might expand your horizons further. But if you have already reached the point at which you have some productive discomfort about how to proceed, then it's time to seek help to work through that discomfort.

This activity will require you to get some assistance from a few other people. If you're already working through this process in a group, rely on those folks. If you're working solo, that's no problem—any thoughtful person can help you with this. They don't need to have prior knowledge of what you're working on, or any special expertise in the subject you're exploring. They don't even need to have detailed knowledge of school librarianship if they are people who you trust to coach your thinking. However you recruit them, you only need to find a few people who can help you get past the "yeah, but..." points where your thinking is stuck.

You'll work within a simple T-chart structure. On the left, list your biggest "yeah, but..." thoughts. Narrow it to your three or four top concerns, if you can, and leave some space between them on the page. Don't try to edit them or solve them at this point! Just record your honest fears and discomforts about the ambitious ideas you're considering. If your concerns are nebulous at this point, just leave them that way—sometimes discomfort isn't clearly diagnosable, and that's natural and okay. However, if you can be more specific, do so. "I'm worried other educators won't have time at the end of the year to collaborate with me on this" will shed a little more light on potential problems (educators' busy schedules and overfull plates, the timing at the end of the school year) than a simple "no one will work with me." The more clarity you are able to bring to your concerns, the better your thought partners will be able to help you with them.

The next step is where your helpers will come in. Leave the right-hand column completely blank. You do not need to come up with solutions right now; that's not your job at this point. If you already knew the solutions to your problems, then they wouldn't be concerning you! Instead, your helpers will read your concerns in the left column and then use the right to suggest some possible solutions. Because they have more distance and less emotional stress attached to the specific focus you're trying to work toward, they will bring fresh eyes and different perspectives to the problems you're trying to solve. This makes them more likely to be able to generate creative and productive solutions that will help you get past your sticking points.

If you are working in a group, it's often useful to have everyone sit in a circle and pass their charts to the person on their right. Set a timer for three minutes (or another duration per the group's choice) and note possible solutions on the chart you receive; then pass to the right again, reset the timer, and repeat this cycle for as many rounds as are needed until you receive your chart back. In this way, everyone in the room will efficiently receive advice from everyone else. If you are not working in a group, simply give your chart to each person helping you and then leave them alone for a few minutes to jot down some suggestions for you. Make sure all of your helpers use the same copy of your chart so that each subsequent person who works on it will be able to see what has already been suggested. That will allow them to be even more creative and helpful by generating new ideas to avoid repeats or to refine suggestions that have already been made.

After you complete this activity and receive notes back from your colleagues, return to your list of possible action steps. Use their feedback and suggestions to improve your action steps by revising ideas or adding details. If you're working in a group and have the chance to give feedback as well as receive it, feel free to use any ideas you may have come up with for someone else to improve your own work. Generating solutions for someone else's sticking points can be exactly the catalyst you need to give your own exploration learning process a boost!

Activity 5: Project Mapping

GETTING ORGANIZED	
Intended outcome:	Flesh out refined action steps into a fully developed plan for professional learning and implementation aligned with the Focus Statement.
You'll need...	• Worksheet for Activity 5: Project Mapping on page **135** • Optional: markers and chart paper or posterboard
Approximate time commitment:	• About 25–30 minutes
Next steps...	• May move on to Activity 6 immediately if desired

After multiple rounds of thinking about what you want to learn in order to strengthen your practice, supplemented by layers of feedback and support from your colleagues, you'll be ready to fully flesh out your plans for exploration as professional learning. This is the time to turn the abstract (and sometimes chaotic) creative thinking you've been doing into a clear and actionable plan for your self-directed PD. Assemble all of your thinking about the focus you've defined, the stakeholders you've considered, and the action steps you've brainstormed and refined. All of this will lead to a cogent Project Map that will serve as a guide to explore your way through this new territory in your professional practice.

Now you'll put together your work from previous activities alongside some new details for how to turn it into action. You may have already been processing some of these new details in the background while working on earlier steps, but writing them out will allow you to encode them and add detail. The more concrete you can make your plans in this stage, the better equipped you'll be to bring your ideas to fruition.

Start by recording the latest iterations of your Focus Statement, the description of your target audience, and your refined action steps. If you now find that any of these elements need further refinement or revision, then by all means, refine away! The feedback and support you've received from your colleagues, plus any marination time you've had since the last activity, have likely brought some additional clarity to your previous thinking. Once you've assembled your best-yet version of those big-picture elements, you can begin fleshing out the details.

Make some decisions about the timeline for implementing your action steps: When will you accomplish each step? What sub-steps will need to happen throughout the year? What other events during the year will impact your implementation? For big action steps, particularly goals or tasks you hope to complete by the end of the year, breaking them down into sub-steps to execute throughout the year will make your work much more manageable. If you're not sure exactly when on the calendar something might happen, describe timing in terms of other benchmarks like "as soon as we find out who our new principal will be" or "after the social studies classes finish their spring semester of standardized testing." Your professional time is your most scarce and valuable resource, so putting effort and attention into writing down a detailed timeline for implementation will be one of your most important tools for bringing your ideas to fruition.

Think forward to your outcome indicators. What signs do you expect to see that will let you know whether your efforts in each action step are working? Leadership gurus often refer to *leading* and *lagging* indicators, both of which you may want to consider. To understand the difference, this analogy may be helpful: leading indicators are like checking for a fever, and lagging indicators are like conducting an autopsy. One shows a small sign early on in the process, and the other shows big, clear signs after everything is done. Both help to understand what happened with a patient's health, so both are valuable and worthwhile. So in terms of your professional learning, let's say you have planned an action step related to improving perceptions of the value of your collaborative work held by other educators in your school. To check leading indicators, you might plan to ask each educator with whom you collaborate during the year a simple check-in question like "what was most valuable to you about the work we've done here?" and keep some notes about their responses. To check lagging indicators, you might send out a more comprehensive end-of-year survey to the whole faculty.

All of the planning work you're doing throughout this exploration is valuable professional learning, and you will learn even more as you start implementing new ideas and adjust your work based on the results, but also consider what specific new knowledge or additional skills you may need to gain independently to succeed at the goals you've made. If you are trying an idea you read about in the Backpack section of this book, do you need to scout out some school libraries near you that are already implementing it? If your plans for enhancing your practice will require you to learn a new technology, do you need to attend a training workshop or enlist the help of a tech coach in your district? If you are hoping to engage a target audience that is different from the groups you've worked with in the past, do you need to broaden your collaborative perspective by researching the things that are most important to them? Plan for what you may not know yet, think through how you can acquire that knowledge, and assign those acquisition tasks to your detailed timeline. This will help you make sure you feel competent and prepared for each action step you want to complete.

Finally, it is helpful to think through and put in writing the mindsets you want to embrace as you complete this work. What will you do or need to remember when the work becomes tough or when you get stuck? If you have planned an ambitious exploration, chances are good that the going will not always be easy. As we've said before in this book, learning is hard work! When you are a dedicated professional and truly care about the quality of your work, it is natural to feel some unpleasant emotions when you're trying something new, especially if it does not go smoothly on the first try. Emotions are awfully slippery and hard to handle in the moment, so your best bet to weather those storms is to shore up your defenses ahead of time, when you are not currently in the middle of those feelings. Giving yourself a catchphrase or credo you can remind yourself of, like "I'm doing this because my learners are worth it," or a go-to person or environment that will help you through a tough day, like "Cry it out with Kayla and a glass of wine, then get back on the horse!," will increase the chances that you'll work through the tough times instead of giving up your exploration and returning to your old way of doing things.

When you've worked through all of the elements in this activity, consider rewriting them in a large format such as on a sheet of chart paper or a posterboard. You'll likely refine your ideas further in the process of rewriting, and you'll end up with a product you can hang on your wall and look at for inspiration throughout your exploration. If you choose to create this large-format document for your project map, you can also add any other elements that suit your methods for thinking and creating. Color-code your action steps for independent versus collaborative work, lay the timeline out as a flow chart with shapes and arrows to show relationships between the various stages of work, decorate the margins to make your planned work feel beautiful and polished, and so on. Go wild and make it your own!

Activity 6: Summative Feedback

GETTING ORGANIZED	
Intended outcome:	Solicit feedback and refine the details of your plan, in order to ensure you're embarking on your best-quality work.
You'll need...	• Worksheet for Activity 6: Summative Feedback on page **137** • Optional: scratch paper
Approximate time commitment:	• About 5 minutes per thought partner • If thought partners are not gathered in a single group, this activity can be spread out over several days in order to meet each thought partner individually, if needed.
Next steps...	• Celebrate the hard work you've done so far! • Go forth and implement your plan!

After completing your project map, you will want to do what you've done throughout this journey of exploration as professional learning: seek feedback! You now have a detailed and refined plan for exactly what learning you want to accomplish to broaden and strengthen your practice. With all of that abstract thinking made into a concrete and coherent map, your friends, colleagues, and stakeholders will be better prepared to support you by helping you make your planned work even better.

I recommend a simple protocol of "Praise, Question, Polish" to gather this feedback. Sticking to this protocol may not feel easy or natural, but it is more efficient than using simple open-ended conversation to learn how to strengthen your work. The procedure is easy to follow: simply ask one or more friends or colleagues to read through your project map and respond in terms of praises, questions, or polishes.

- **Praise:** Praises are exactly what they sound like. Your reviewers will note the parts of your plans that they think are particularly strong or commendable.
- **Question:** Your reviewers may ask you to clarify parts of your work that are still abstract or need more detail, or they can inquire about your reasons for a particular step or element in the plan.
- **Polish:** Polishes may consist of advice on how to better reach a segment of your target audience, possible opportunities for new learning that you may not have known about, polite disagreement or pushback on an action step that will need some adjustment in order to work well, or any other areas that will help strengthen your work.

Ideally, seek out several different people for feedback; each pair of eyes that looks at your project map will offer a different perspective, all of which will help you further refine your work. You can then sort out the feedback you've received into a scheme that makes sense to you—perhaps you'd find it helpful to separate the praises, questions, and polishes, or maybe you'd like to organize the suggestions into what you should adjust now versus what you'll consider later—and begin to work it into your plans for action.

You will always have more chances to make further changes later if necessary, even if you realize something new once implementation is under way! This work belongs wholly to you, and you retain the ultimate right and responsibility for "iteratively responding to challenges" (AASL 2018, Learner V.D.1.) as you move toward implementation.

ACTIVITY 1

Self-Assessment

Describe your two to three most important outcomes for each of these audiences:

Desired Outcomes for Learners:	%
Desired Outcomes with Educators:	%
Desired Outcomes for the School Community:	%

Next, describe your current outputs in each of these categories:

Productive and Social Relationships:	%	Environment and Infrastructure:	%
Stakeholder Perceptions of the School Library:	%	Core Values in School Librarianship:	%

After making qualitative notes in all seven lenses, complete your self-assessment with a quantitative analysis by assigning a percentage score indicating how close your current practice comes to your ideal vision in each area.

ACTIVITY 2

Focus Definition

First, use this space to sketch a visual representation of your strengths, growth areas, and their intersections:

Next, convert your visual representation into targeted, concise notes on your most current thinking in each of these categories:

High Priority Needs	High Leverage Learning	Personal Strengths

continued on next page

ACTIVITY 2

Focus Definition *(continued)*

Finally, draft a narrow Focus Statement following this template:

I want to learn and implement______________, so that ________________ outcome(s) will be possible. I will be able to accomplish this goal by (choose one of the following:) learning to _______________, developing a partnership with _______________, and/or becoming better aligned with ____________________.

My draft Focus Statement:

ACTIVITY 3

Action Steps

Start by recording the most current version of your Focus Statement. Next, describe the target audience you hope to serve with this work, then brainstorm possible action steps to serve them.

Focus Statement:
Target Audience:
Possible Action Steps:

ACTIVITY 4

Problems and Solutions

Start by recording the most current version of your Focus Statement. Next, use the left column to record the biggest "yeah, but..." concerns you have with your current action steps. Ask several thought partners to use the right column to suggest possible solutions for each concern.

Focus Statement:	
Problems What issues or sticking points do you foresee with the action steps you've generated?	**Solutions** What may be some possible solutions?

ACTIVITY 5

Project Mapping

Map your thinking for how to accomplish your learning goals. Reiterate your Focus Statement, target audience, and action steps. Then add full implementation details by assigning a timeline to your action steps, planning the outcome indicators you expect to see, determining what new learning you will need during the course of this work, and establishing the mindsets that will support you through successful execution.

Focus Statement:
Target Audience:
Action Steps:

continued on next page

ACTIVITY 5

Project Mapping *(continued)*

Timeline:
Outcome Indicators:
New Learning Needed:
Mindsets:

ACTIVITY 6

Summative Feedback

Seek feedback on your project map from one or more colleagues. Use the spaces below to record and organize the feedback you receive.

Praise:
Question:
Polish:

10

The Journey to Implementation

Congratulations! You should now have an excellent start on a concrete and well thought-out action plan for pursuing ambitious transformations in your professional practice. This by itself is an important accomplishment: engaging in strategic planning is very difficult, especially under the constraints of time and energy that school employees face. But even beyond that, you have worked through a complex and vulnerable process of professional learning via exploration, modeling some of the same Competencies that the Explore standards require of the learners in our school communities.

Model of Professional Learning

Let's take a reflective look back at some of the ways Competencies in the Shared Foundation of Explore have appeared in your learning process.

QUESTIONING AND REFLECTION

Professional learning will always imply change, and the early activities in this guide are about focusing and defining that change—thereby "reflecting and questioning assumptions and possible misconceptions" (AASL 2018, Learner V.A.2.) about the work we've been doing previously. The process of assessing your current practice and comparing it against your vision in **Activity 1: Self-Assessment** invited you to question your assumptions about how your current everyday work aligns with the outcomes you want to see as a result of it. **Activity 4: Problems and Solutions** challenged you to question your assumptions and possible misconceptions about what is possible in your program by asking colleagues to generate solutions to your "yeah, but..." points.

All professionals already do the best work they believe they can do, every day. So to engage in a learning process, wherein we select a focus for growth and begin to tackle it, is to question our assumptions about what we've previously believed we were capable of. And any time we discover we have been mistaken about our limits, it's a beautiful thing!

LEARNING BY DESIGN

The Planning Guide is based on the principles of design thinking and project-based learning. Completing it in full and implementing your plan will essentially walk you through "problem solving through cycles of design, implementation, and reflection" (AASL 2018, Learner V.B.1.) as a complete cycle that has reflection built in at multiple steps along the way. **Activity 1: Self-Assessment** can be compared to the Empathize stage of design thinking (figure 10.1), wherein you examine and assess where your work is now and what you want your outcomes to be so that you can fully understand the function of what your resulting plan needs to be. **Activity 2: Focus Definition** can be compared to the Define stage, wherein you bring clarity and concision to your choices about the learning work you are undertaking in service of your desired outcomes. **Activity 3: Action Steps** can be compared to the Ideate stage, wherein you generate a variety of ideas that might help you reach your desired outcomes, sorting through and selecting the best of those ideas, and proactively generating solutions to some of the barriers you may encounter. **Activity 5: Project Mapping** can be compared to the Prototype stage, wherein you flesh out the details of the innovative practice or programmatic shift you intend to implement. **Activity 4: Problems and Solutions** and **Activity 6: Summative Feedback** can be compared to the Test stage, wherein you seek feedback on your prototype plans and refine them to make them stronger.

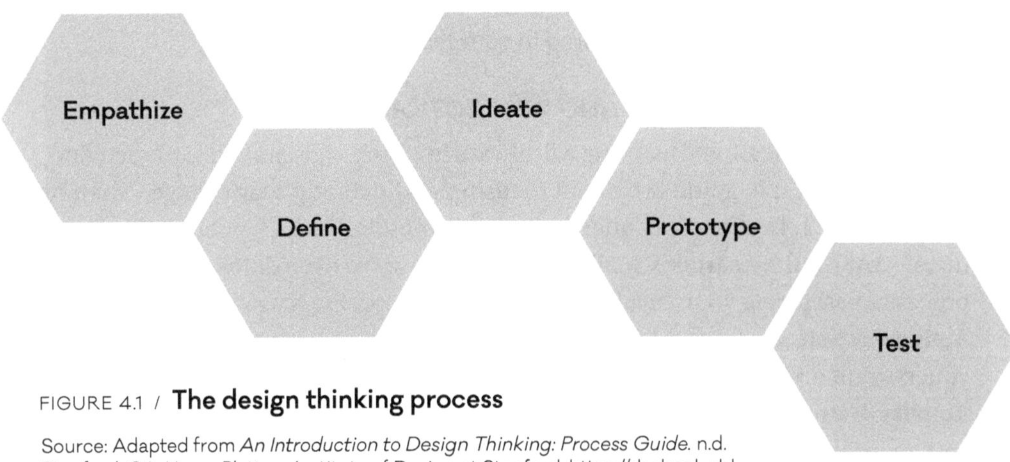

FIGURE 4.1 / **The design thinking process**

Source: Adapted from *An Introduction to Design Thinking: Process Guide.* n.d. Stanford, CA: Hasso Plattner Institute of Design at Stanford. https://dschool-old.stanford.edu/sandbox/groups/designresources/wiki/36873/attachments/74b3d/ModeGuideBOOTCAMP2010L.pdf.

At all stages, you are invited to seek feedback through conversations with colleagues so that you can reflect on your work and iteratively improve your ideas.

AMBITIOUS INNOVATION

If, in your process of completing the Planning Guide, there was no point at which you became tired, frustrated, or daunted by the enormity of the work you were attempting to undertake, then I suggest you go back and try again! As professional learners, we are tasked to take Explore's directive for "persisting through self-directed pursuits by tinkering and making" (AASL 2018, Learner V.B.2.) seriously. Self-directed work, like the professional learning required to transform and innovate in your school library practice, is ambitious and requires persistence and grit to complete. If there were easy answers to the complex problems of practice that school librarians face when trying to better serve their learners and school communities, then some smart person would already have figured them out and prescribed them to the rest of us, thus eliminating the need for the type of self-directed pursuit that you've undertaken. But that is not the case. Because each school librarian's needs and goals are unique, because each school's learners, communities, conditions, constraints, and opportunities are unique, personalized self-directed learning is really the only path forward—and it requires tremendous persistence on your part to move along that path.

It's important to recognize that your implementation plan, drafted in detail in **Activity 5: Project Mapping**, is a "made" thing. It may not look beautiful or polished, or even tangible, but it is a thing that did not exist before you made it, and that makes your planning process an act of creation. The work you do to implement it will be a further act of making. As you've improved your ideas at every stage of the planning process, and as you'll continue to improve them during implementation and future refinement, you've been tinkering with your creation. Many people are tempted to believe that tinkering and making only count when they result in handheld crafts or models, but the truth is that making is a mindset and a pursuit that applies to what you've undertaken in your planning process.

COLLABORATIVE PROBLEM SOLVING

This Planning Guide was adapted from the structure of the in-person professional development workshops I lead, and as discussed in the introductions to the various activities, ideally most of it is done with partners or in a group setting. Explore's Competency for "collaboratively identifying innovative solutions to a challenge or problem" (AASL 2018, Learner V.C.3.) is the reason for that. When you work through ambitious and important problems of practice in collaboration with trusted colleagues, you are much more likely to identify innovative solutions than you would have been able to design on your own. Knowledge is socially constructed; humans are built to learn together, both from and alongside each other. Even if you weren't able to gather a formal group to work through the process in full alongside you, each time you asked someone to give you feedback on an activity will have dramatically increased your ability to innovate and solve problems more elegantly and productively.

CONTINUAL REFINEMENT THROUGH ITERATION

If you are like most of the people who have participated in the in-person workshops that this Planning Guide is based on, then your first reaction to some of the activities may have been that they seem awfully repetitive—but your later reaction was probably to notice that every time you thought you were done with your plan, it turned out there was more to it. In an iterative cycle, each stage asks you to dig deeper, think differently, and create more. When we are engaged in "iteratively responding to challenges" (AASL 2018, Learner V.D.1.), our practice grows stronger.

The value in iteration is the reason many inquiry models, including the design thinking that this Planning Guide is based on, are referred to as "cycles." As discussed in more detail in chapter 4, inquiry learning will always be a somewhat messy and nonlinear process. By spiraling around to look at your work from a variety of different angles and with a variety of different activity protocols, testing a concept and adjusting your thinking and then testing it again, your work through the Planning Guide harnessed an iterative structure to help you navigate that cognitive mess. By cycling through your challenges multiple times, you were able to extract more value out of your planning process than if you'd tried to sit down and think through it only once in a linear fashion.

When you really think iteration through, you may notice the obvious problem for busy adults, which is that cycles make it very difficult to tell when you are finished! The bad news is that the answer is probably "never." But the good news is that every time we iterate and make changes to improve our practice, our learners and school communities benefit. Evergreen growth is what puts the "professional" in our role as professional learners.

GROWING THROUGH FEEDBACK

The Planning Guide is ideally completed in a group setting for collaborative purposes but also for feedback purposes. Many of the activities invite you to engage in conversations with your colleagues and partners, which will likely result in feedback that helps you refine your thinking, and some activities explicitly require you to seek out that feedback. As professional learners, "open-mindedly accepting feedback for positive and constructive growth" (AASL 2018, Learner V.D.3.) is where our most powerful gains are found.

Depending on your comfort level with the topic area you selected for implementation and your relationships with the colleagues giving you feedback, you may or may not have felt the "open-mindedly accepting" clause of this Competency. It is one thing to accept feedback we agree with or find easy to deal with, but it is much more difficult to be open-minded when the feedback we receive might prompt significant redirection in our work. Learning necessarily implies some kind of change, and ambitious learning implies significant change; therefore, if you chose to pursue ambitious learning, it is possible that you may have encountered feedback you did not enjoy receiving. Change is a vulnerable process, even when we truly believe it is the right thing to do, and feedback related to it is not always easy or pleasant. The key to receiving it open-mindedly and constructively is positive and trusting relationships with your partners. Strong relationships with those working alongside you can shore up the vulnerability you may feel in your role as a learner. Creating an environment conducive to these effective relationships is one of the most important things you can do to set up your professional learning experience to be successful.

Final Steps of a Long Journey

When you reach the end of a complex process like the professional learning you have just undertaken, I strongly recommend you engage in a step that is missing from many PD scenarios: celebrate it! Any sort of celebration is appropriate if it is meaningful to you. Here are a few ideas to get you started:

- **Share your work:** Write a letter to your school administrator or another leader in your school community that tells them about your learning process and your upcoming plans to integrate that learning for the benefit of other learners in the school.
- **Invite others to fellowship:** Treat yourself to a snack or drink with a colleague who understands the importance of what you've been working on.
- **Present your learning:** Submit proposals to present your work and describe your learning process at a conference or other professional event.
- **Keep it visible:** Make a poster or other visual of your work that you can hang above your desk to remind you of your success and inspire you in the future.

Most important of all, celebrate your Planning Guide success by putting all of your hard planning work into action. Remember: what you've been planning for is what you intend to *do*. So even though the planning and learning have been quite a bit of work already, resist the temptation to slow down and leave the plan on paper! The greatest rewards in learning, for us as well as for our student learners, are intrinsic. The truest celebration of what you've learned will come when you see your transformed and innovative work making a positive difference in the lives of your learners, collaborating educators, and other members of your school community.

COMPASS CHECK

Questions for the Reflective Practitioner

1. How does it feel to play the role of a learner? What are your intellectual, physical, and emotional reactions to working through this exploration process?
2. How can your own experience exploring ideas as a learner shed light on what your student learners experience while exploring in your school library and in the rest of the school?
3. Based on your experience as a learner, what elements in your school library instruction, environment, collaboration, or programming might you want to adjust in order to make sure all your learners are able to explore effectively?

Conclusion: Landmarks in the Shared Foundations

This book opened with a metaphor—Compass, Backpack, and Boots— about what things are necessary to Explore. It is my sincere hope that after reading this book, you now feel better equipped for your professional journey with this Shared Foundation. But real journeys are complicated, and as with any real-life exploration, this one won't stop with the equipment you're carrying. As you move and work, you'll interact with the whole environment that surrounds you. On occasion, that environment can get so complicated and messy that it can obscure the path you've intended to follow! A few landmarks are helpful for making sense of the wider world and clarifying where you are and where you want to be. We'll close this book by looking for those landmarks among the other five Shared Foundations.

Inquire

The Shared Foundation of Inquire connects naturally to Explore when, as learners, we find something through our explorations that we want to bite into and pursue further. Indeed, if we weren't paying close attention, it would be easy enough to look at the Key Commitment for Inquire to "build new knowledge by inquiring, thinking critically, identifying problems, and developing strategies for solving problems" (AASL 2018, 68) and assume it was another Explore Competency! If we were to compare Explore to a glacial lake—big, beautiful, with ripples on the surface and depths below—then it would be easy to see Inquire as a stream originating from the lake and gradually building into river rapids. This conceit lets us see how Explore offers a wide-open and deep range of possibilities for learners' interests, and Inquire as giving those interests a direction and flow, using the riverbanks as defined boundaries to narrow their breadth but extend their length and momentum.

In Inquire, the AASL Standards call on learners to formulate questions about personal interests (AASL 2018, Learner I.A.1.), generate products that illustrate learning (AASL 2018, Learner I.B.3.), act on feedback to improve (AASL 2018, Learner I.C.3.), and engage in sustained inquiry (AASL 2018, Learner I.D.2.). All of these things, as well as others among the Inquire Competencies, are directly related to Explore's demands for learners to inquire, make, and iterate in the pursuits of personal curiosity and growth. As discussed in chapter 4, the Explore Competencies are how we nurture natural curiosity. The Inquire Competencies are how we systematically respond to that curiosity and channel it into new learning, both for personal and academic growth. When these two Shared Foundations are taken together and implemented well, the result will be critical thinking dispositions that permeate the school learning community and reinforce the school library's role in "maximizing learning, creating new knowledge and institutional effectiveness" (AASL 2018, 73).

The two Shared Foundations are tightly aligned, and everyday implementation of one is highly likely to end up involving pieces of the other. For instance, if we've worked with learners on a self-assessment to recognize how their current skill sets can be improved and expanded (AASL 2018, Learner V.D.2.), then we'll certainly want to follow that by helping them make a plan to fill their knowledge gaps (AASL 2018, Learner I.B.2.) and act on feedback to improve (AASL 2018, Learner I.C.3.). If we're developing opportunities for learners to share their products with an authentic audience (AASL 2018, Learner I.C.4.), then we'll want to support that by co-constructing an innovative investigation (AASL 2018, Learner V.C.2.) that they can take pride in showing off. And if we guide them effectively to read widely and deeply (AASL 2018, Learner V.A.1.), we'll be deepening the well they draw on for recalling prior knowledge as context for new meaning (AASL 2018, Learner I.A.2.). When school librarians carefully look for these tight connections between Explore and Inquire, using them in tandem will dramatically increase our ability to effectively grow and reinforce these competencies among our learners.

Include

The Shared Foundation of Include connects to Explore when we start to consider all the different viewpoints learners' explorations may expose them to, either in digital and print resources or through interaction with other learners. If we've compared Explore and Inquire to bodies of water, then it's fair to continue the nature metaphors with the other Shared Foundations too! Include, then, is the ecosystem we might find in that glacial lake and around its banks. It includes a complex system of living and changing creatures who interact with each other and with their environment, wherein the success of the whole system depends on those interactions staying balanced. When learners follow Include's Key Commitment to "demonstrate an understanding of and commitment to inclusiveness and respect for diversity in the learning community" (AASL 2018, 76), they are acting as caretakers and conservators of the many beautiful and fascinating forms of life they will encounter while exploring.

All of Explore's work supporting learners' individual interests and passions must be balanced with responsibility toward the others around them who are trying to do the same things. When the new learning we're exploring is meaningful, the process of investigating it takes us outside of our current comfort levels or immediate environments, and that means entering territory with new voices and viewpoints. To conduct explorations effectively, learners must become strongly empathetic and responsive to those voices and viewpoints, which is what the Competencies in Include are there to support. Include prompts us to use what we're exploring to make our world better for everyone.

Everyday implementation of Explore will always be richer and more meaningful if it is coupled with implementation of Include. For instance, the work of iteratively responding to challenges (AASL 2018, Learner V.D.1.) requires learners to evaluate their own work and improve it, and they will evaluate themselves more effectively when they can reflect on their own place within the global learning community (AASL 2018, Learner II.D.3.). Doing so allows learners to see how their work compares to what others have done, matching or rubbing against their expectations and experiences, so that they can accept feedback for positive and constructive growth (AASL 2018, Learner V.D.3.), especially if they have engaged in informed conversations and active debate (AASL 2018, Learner II.C.1.) along the way. Particularly when a learner's tinkering and making are formalized into cycles of design and implementation that are intended to solve a problem (AASL 2018, Learner V.B.1.), their learning will be strongly impacted by interacting with others who reflect a range of perspectives (AASL 2018, Learner II.B.1.)—because otherwise, for whom are they solving that problem, and how will they know whether their solution is successful? As school librarians, when we lead any type of activity or programming, we have an imperative to ensure that diverse voices and perspectives are honored. Systematic inclusion makes exploration more powerful.

Collaborate

If Explore is like a glacial lake, and Include is like the ecosystem in and around that lake, then Collaborate can be understood as a very specific part of that ecosystem—the human part. Many parts of nature depend on each other to survive and thrive, but relatively few are actively and intentionally working together to bring about positive outcomes. If we start to envision our lakeside scene with humans erecting a small fishing village, we'll see how its members "work effectively with others to broaden perspectives and work toward common goals," as the Key Commitment for Collaborate asks our learners to do (AASL 2018, 85). Collaboration is what allows us not just to live, but to grow new abilities and achieve things that are not possible for individuals working alone.

As much as the Explore Competencies lend themselves to personalized pursuits, the true depth of possibilities in Explore are unlikely to be realized by one learner in isolation. They can't. The AASL Standards are grounded in the body of research-based educational theory, one pillar of which is that learning is socially constructed. When Explore asks learners to co-construct innovative means of investigation (AASL 2018, Learner V.C.2.), collaboratively identify innovative solutions to a challenge or problem (AASL 2018, Learner V.C.3.), and open-mindedly accept feedback for positive and constructive growth (AASL 2018, Learner V.D.3.), those learners' interdependence with their peers becomes as clear as glacial waters. The connections between Explore and Collaborate, then, highlight how working together with others doesn't detract from the pursuit of personal curiosity, but is what actually makes that work possible.

In everyday implementation, all Explore Competencies—not only the ones that necessitate it—will be benefitted by connecting with Collaborate Competencies. Learners will be more successful at engaging in inquiry-based processes for personal growth (AASL 2018, Learner V.A.3.) when they involve diverse perspectives in their own inquiry processes (AASL 2018, Learner III.C.2.). Learners are most likely to reflect and question assumptions and possible misconceptions (AASL 2018, Learner V.A.2.) when they are developing new understandings through engagement in a learning group (AASL 2018, Learner III.A.2.). Even when learners persist through self-directed pursuits by tinkering and making (AASL 2018, Learner V.B.2.), they'll do their best work when they are soliciting and responding to feedback from others (AASL 2018, Learner III.C.1.) to improve their products. Collaboration is not the special province of the occasional big group project; it is the best way humans learn as they Explore in any context.

Curate

The Shared Foundation of Curate is best seen as connected to Explore not as something inherent within it, but as something that informs how we make choices about approaching it. So in our metaphorical nature scene, Curate might be compared to a through-hiker on the Appalachian Trail who revels in the glacial lake while camping by it, using her carefully selected supplies. The hiker must be relentlessly thoughtful about what supplies she chooses to carry, because each tool adds to the weight of her pack and therefore to the difficulty of her journey. Every item in the pack has to accomplish a purpose that is necessary, not tangential, to the hiker's success; ideally, each item is specialized to that purpose in the context of hiking, a best-of-breed item that will significantly improve the hiker's experience by its inclusion. The pack is not the point of the hike—no one sets out on the Appalachian Trail because they can't wait to haul around a forty-pound backpack for six months—but it's what makes it possible for the hiker to accomplish her purpose of reaching locations like the lake. Following the Key Commitment of Curate, to "make meaning for oneself and others by collecting, organizing, and sharing resources of personal relevance," enables learners to Explore (AASL 2018, 94).

When learners Explore, they encounter numerous and iterative needs to have their process informed by a variety of resources. The Learner Domains ask learners to develop and satisfy personal curiosity, construct new knowledge, engage with the learning community, and develop themselves through experience and reflection—all of which invites the question: about what? What should learners be curious about, what should their newly constructed knowledge be about, and so on? That "what" indicates the central role of high-quality resources in the learning process, and Curate is how we connect learners to the resources they need. As well, we can easily ask the reverse question: if Curate asks learners to act on information needs, gather information, exchange information resources, and select and organize information for a variety of audiences, what for? What tasks should those processes inform? Explore helps define what learners can begin to do with the resources they've gathered.

Everyday implementation of either Explore or Curate will therefore tend to look like the two sides of a coin. If learners express curiosity about a topic of personal interest or curricular relevance (AASL 2018, Learner V.C.1.), it naturally follows that that curiosity determines a need to gather information and that they'll want to begin identifying possible sources (AASL 2018, Learner IV.A.1 and IV.A.2.). When learners access and evaluate collaboratively constructed information sites (AASL 2018, Learner IV.C.1.), their reflective responses to that evaluation should lead them to recognize their own capabilities and skills that can be developed, improved, and expanded (AASL 2018, Learner V.D.2.). In order for learners to iteratively respond to challenges (AASL 2018, Learner V.D.1.), they'll need to integrate their conceptual understanding gained from resources (AASL 2018, Learner IV.D.2.) before they can effectively make their next steps. Done right, the continual interplay of Explore and Curate creates a feedback loop for lifelong learning.

Engage

The Shared Foundation of Engage perfectly sums up how a learner will Explore responsibly. With one last look at the metaphorical nature scene we've been building, the best place to see Engage is in the way the through-hikers interact as they move along the trail. All of them are moving at individual paces and for their own unique purposes, but by using the trail, they accept common responsibilities to share news and weather updates with their fellow hikers, clean up their campsites to care for the environment, and avoid feeding the bears. When learners follow the Key Commitment of Engage to "demonstrate safe, legal, and ethical creating and sharing of knowledge products independently while engaging in a community of practice and an interconnected world" (AASL 2018, 113), they affirm that their personal learning is situated in an outward-facing context, and that the impact of their exploration on others should be positive and responsible.

The Competencies in Explore are heavily personalized, designed to support learners in developing ownership over their lifelong learning, and at first glance it would be easy to read them as individual processes. By connecting Explore with Engage, however, we build an understanding that all of those personalized processes are situated in a collective context, and that each learner's explorations are part of the larger fabric of the learning community. At all points when we engage in personalized pursuits, we are responsible to consider how our actions affect others and how we can ensure we're making positive contributions that will lift the whole group. Engage gives us the guidance we need to do that.

We can think of everyday implementation of Engage as an extension of Explore by consistently making it a habit of learning to consider how our work is part of a greater whole. When learners use resources and collaborate as they engage in inquiry-based processes for personal growth (AASL 2018, Learner V.A.3.), they must acknowledge authorship and demonstrate respect for the intellectual property of others (AASL 2018, Learner VI.B.2.). When they co-construct innovative means of investigation (AASL 2018, Learner V.C.2.), they should inspire their partners to engage in safe, responsible, ethical, and legal information behaviors (AASL 2018, Learner VI.D.3.). And when they create personal knowledge products as they persist through self-directed pursuits by tinkering and making (AASL 2018, Learner V.B.2.), they contribute most effectively when they include elements that allow others to credit that content appropriately (AASL 2018, Learner VI.B.3.). This interdependence between learners and the wider learning community as they Explore and Engage is what truly creates the natural beauty of a well-balanced and interconnected knowledge ecosystem.

Final Thoughts

As explorers, it's inevitable that our paths, no matter how carefully chosen, will eventually encounter hills, streams, or other unexpected variations in the landscape. When that happens, there is no need to fear that we are suddenly on a whole new journey. Even when a natural disaster may pose significant difficulties or setbacks, that doesn't move the needle of our Compass or change our intended destinations. Instead, these variations and setbacks give us reason to pause and regroup, reexamine our priorities, and determine whether we currently still have the tools to break through and follow our original paths. If that's not the case, then it is our responsibility as professionals not to give up and go home, but to figure out how to acquire or even make new tools. Occasionally we'll end up realizing that an ambitious journey will carry us through uncharted territory; if that is the case, then as leaders our job is to blaze the trail so that eventually others following us can traverse it more easily.

As school librarians, we cannot divorce our work from the context in which it is conducted, and so there will always be competing pressures on it. As members of larger school communities, we will find ourselves chasing accountability targets, the shifting priorities of school and district administrators, the whims of elected officials seeking media attention, and the inadequacies of social infrastructure that leave some learners without food and safe shelter. And those are only the variations in our job that can be anticipated! Once in a great while, a truly unprecedented challenge will come along—the COVID-19 global pandemic comes to mind—that has the potential to shake us to our foundations and make us question whether we really know what our work is supposed to be anymore.

But again, as professionals and leaders, it is our responsibility not to give up when these pressures drag us off course from our intended route. There are so many tools available to us to accomplish our goals! First among them is the AASL Standards, which serve as our Compass for where we and our learners need to be headed. After that come the plethora of concepts and areas of content knowledge that inform and enrich the work of schools and school librarianship, a few of which are detailed in this book's Backpack. If none of those reveal the answers we need, then we can begin tinkering and making, using all of those resources to rework and reuse and remix until we create entirely new solutions to benefit our learners and keep our school libraries pointed in the direction we know they need to go. It will not be easy work—in fact, like literal trailblazing, it's likely to be dirty, sweaty, and distinctly unglamorous work—but it is what our learners and our school communities deserve.

By entering the field of school librarianship, we have given ourselves the gift of a career steeped in lifelong learning. What a privilege it is to earn a living by seeking new knowledge and by apprenticing the learners around us to do the same! Even when the context makes this journey terribly tough going, it is the stuff of dreams and legends to be professional explorers. And every time we strap on our Boots to turn our new knowledge into action, we engage in an act of shining optimism that others will profoundly benefit from our labors. As we Think, Create, Share, and Grow in our work, we Explore to make the world a better place.

APPENDIX A

Navigating the Explore Competencies

As described in the introduction, this book's outside-in approach is designed to support librarians by showing how a wide variety of content and ideas in school librarianship can be found within the AASL Standards, specifically within the Shared Foundation of Explore. The intention is to cut down on the "one more thing on our plates" feeling that is so prevalent among educators of all disciplines, which can make any new learning feel overwhelming to get started on.

However, as well-intentioned as that approach may be, it does necessarily involve abandoning any pretense at covering the Explore Competencies in the order they appear in the AASL Standards! If your own professional learning journey is well served by methodically making sure you've studied each Competency, moving inside-out from the Learner, School Librarian, and School Library Frameworks to other content, please see the following chart as a navigation aid. For each Competency and Alignment in the Explore Integrated Framework, the chart points to the chapter of this book in which it is explicitly addressed.

Consider this chart a starting point. School librarianship is complex work, and so there is quite often overlap in how the tools in our Backpacks appear in Explore, just as there is overlap in how various areas of our practice may appear in more than one Shared Foundation. The more experience you gain in implementing Explore and the rest of the AASL Standards, the more subtlety you'll see in how each Competency may appear in an effective school library.

SHARED FOUNDATION V: EXPLORE			
	Learner	**School Librarian**	**School Library**
A. Think	1. Chapter 1 2. Chapters 4, 10 3. Chapter 4	1. Chapter 1 2. Chapter 4 3. Chapter 4	1. Chapter 4 2. Chapters 1, 6
B. Create	1. Chapters 6, 10 2. Chapters 6, 10	1. Chapter 6 2. Chapter 6 3. Chapter 6	1. Chapters 2, 7 2. Chapters 1, 3 3. Chapters 2, 3
C. Share	1. Chapter 7 2. Chapter 4 3. Chapters 7, 10	1. Chapter 7 2. Chapter 4 3. Chapter 7	1. Chapter 5 2. Chapter 1 3. Chapter 3
D. Grow	1. Chapters 4, 10 2. Chapter 5 3. Chapters 7, 10	1. Chapter 4 2. Chapter 5 3. Chapter 7	1. Chapters 2, 5 2. Chapter 3 3. Chapters 2, 5

Workshopping the Explore Planning Guide

The activities in the Explore Planning Guide were born from professional development workshops I have led in my own district, and you may desire to implement them with a group of learners in a workshop format as well. My aim has been to design the Planning Guide in such a way that any individual or loosely formed group can work through the cycle, but if your local community of practice has the capacity to run it as a more formal workshop, you may find that especially productive and positive! This section includes a few tips for workshopping that may help you in your planning process.

Although these tips are aimed at an audience of adult learners, you absolutely can and should consider adapting them to use with student learners engaged in exploration! All learners need and deserve structured support for social construction of new knowledge in an emotionally and intellectually safe environment. By participating in a workshop that models these principles through completing the Planning Guide, school librarians will be better equipped to design safe, rigorous, and successful experiences for all the learners in their school communities.

Tip 1: Structure Conversations

Learning is socially constructed, so conversation is one of the best things we can do for our cognitive development to work on complex problems. Each activity, and even each part of an activity, will therefore be improved by an opportunity to pause and talk about it. However, not all talk is created equal in terms of productively facilitating learning. As a workshop leader, you'll want to add some structure around conversations, to help make sure each opportunity to talk will lead the learning work forward.

Conversational structures can be short and simple. For instance, **Activity 2: Focus Definition** has three categories; a workshop could include a brief turn-and-talk or table share-out after each of the three. The structure to be imposed is a) to insert conversation into the points where it's most needed so that the talk provides cognitive processing directly related to the work being done, and b) to put a time limit on the sharing so that lengthy chats don't end up sapping energy and momentum from the task at hand.

Opportunities for structured conversation can also be more elaborate. One of my favorite workshop debrief activities is an abbreviated partner coaching protocol with two rules: talk about one person's work at a time, and as that person is sharing their thoughts, their partner should respond *only* by paraphrasing or asking questions, so that the partner is helping the sharer clarify and refine their own thinking rather than injecting outside advice. Imposing simple boundaries on conversation using a protocol like this ensures that the talk serves a goal, rather than simply socializing or devolving into venting.

Conversations bounded by structures and protocols are best for efficiently directing talk toward devising solutions, and unbounded conversations are best for quickly releasing mental tension and clarifying thinking in small chunks. A mix of conversation types throughout the workshop will generate different types of thinking and help participants to continually refresh their ideas. Returning to the example of **Activity 2: Focus Definition**, a simple turn-and-talk could be used after each of the first two segments, and the more in-depth partner coaching protocol could be used after the third segment to support participants' full synthesis.

Tip 2: Create Emotional and Intellectual Safety

If participants are committed to in-depth professional learning and growth, then this type of planning will entail some degree of change in practice, and that can be a mighty emotional, as well as a cognitive, lift. Professionals take pride in their work, and it is an inherently vulnerable process to look for places to change and improve. As a workshop leader, you'll need to support them by creating an environment of emotional and intellectual safety, and conversation opportunities can be an excellent tool for this. Look for opportunities to pause and prompt emotional processing with the same methods you'd use to support thinking. For instance, a turn-and-talk during **Activity 1: Self-Assessment** could be a good chance for participants to discuss what they feel proud or passionate about in their work, or to reflect on which parts of their honest quantitative assessments make them feel excited and which make them feel nervous. I strongly recommend that vulnerable emotional processing is better done in very small groups rather than sharing with everyone!

Another way to create emotional and intellectual safety is to lean on existing norms and address existing needs within the group. You know your participants better than anyone else— trust your instincts! If you believe they'll feel more comfortable doing this work as a retreat in a community room at a coffee shop instead of a dedicated professional development room in a school building, then by all means, book the coffee shop! If the district is encouraging all its educators to use Socratic circles and gallery walks during student learning activities, then consider adapting **Activity 4: Problems and Solutions** into a Socratic circle, and use a gallery walk to structure **Activity 6: Summative Feedback**, so that these activities can double as models for them to imitate in their own instruction. Tailoring the workshop to their specific needs will help them have a terrific experience.

Tip 3: Work the Whole Process

Though tailoring a workshop to local needs is important and appropriate, I do recommend sticking as closely as possible to the skeleton of the Planning Guide's structure, and not trying to skip or alter any of the activity parts. Some parts of the process can feel difficult or uncomfortable; for instance, many school librarians find it challenging to think through leading and lagging indicators in **Activity 5: Project Mapping**. That is because it is inherently challenging work, not because school librarians are not capable of accomplishing it!

People are naturally reticent about painstakingly digging through ambitious new ideas, so some parts of this process will feel unnatural and uncomfortable on the first try. But that's exactly why all activities should be executed with fidelity to the process. If the activities all felt natural and comfortable, we'd all already be doing that type of thinking every day, and we wouldn't need a workshop or Planning Guide to help us. As when we lead our student learners through an inquiry cycle informed by a research-based framework, the structure is designed to help us be successful.

Tip 4: Provide Think-alouds

The ambitious work conducted in the Planning Guide can be challenging—once again, if it were easy and comfortable, everyone would already be doing it and we wouldn't need a structure to help us—and participants may find examples helpful. There are advantages and disadvantages to providing high-quality exemplars of how learners should approach difficult or complex work. The big advantage, of course, is that exemplars clarify the expectations for work. They illustrate exactly the type of performance the instructions are meant to convey, they show the appropriate level of depth or detail to strive for, and they can help learners feel more confident about how to approach the task before them. The big disadvantage, however, is that narrowing participants' vision to emulate a "correct" example can cut off the creative and divergent thinking that professional learning through exploration is intended to entail. For this reason, I have not included completed samples of the activity worksheets in this book, and I have been sparing in the examples I've given within the text.

However, during workshops, you have a middle-ground option for supporting participants' work: the think-aloud. As part of introducing activities, a think-aloud gives you a chance to orally model the type of thinking you expect participants to be doing for themselves. Think-alouds offer the type of clarity that are advantageous in exemplars, without locking in to a concrete exemplar that might lead participants to imitate it rather than doing their own cognitive exploration. I like to offer think-alouds about my own work supporting school librarians, so that it's close-to-home enough that they can understand the process I'm modeling but far enough from their actual practice so that they won't be tempted to let it lead their own thinking. For instance, in helping participants describe their target audiences as part of **Activity 3: Action Steps**, I might describe how I had thought about the different levels of professional experience among the school librarians who might be attending that workshop so that I could plan activities to support their varied needs. This would allow me to explicitly model how much depth of information to include in this part of the activity, while ensuring that I have not influenced the way they do the activity.

Tip 5: Allow Plenty of Time

Workshopping through the whole Explore Planning Guide will take some time. Again, if this were quick work, we'd all already be doing it. Trying to rush through it will cheapen and flatten the thinking it requires. In my district, I find it takes about nine hours to work through all six activity stages while allowing ample time for conversation and collaboration. Of the workshops I've led, my favorite was a summer professional development week that took eighteen hours (six hours each on Monday, Wednesday, and Friday) that had content sessions similar to this book's Backpack interspersed between the strategic planning activities represented in this Planning Guide.

If possible, I recommend scheduling your workshop during the summer or at other times when your participants aren't on contract time in their buildings, rather than trying to spread out the nine hours across after-school sessions. After-school sessions can work in a pinch, because sometimes that's the only option we have available—but remember that this is hard work, and it gets even harder if participants are exhausted from a work day before they even get started! It's also helpful to break the workshop into several chunks if you can, rather than scheduling a single marathon nine-hour day, because the opportunity to sleep between activities is powerful for participants' refining and improving their work. A series of three half-days is a happy medium if you can swing it.

Works Cited

AASL American Association of School Librarians. 2018. "Definition of an Effective School Library." www.ala.org/aasl/sites/ala.org.aasl/files/content/advocacy/statements/docs/AASL_Position_Statement_Effective_SLP_2018.pdf

———. 2018. *National School Library Standards for Learners, School Librarians, and School Libraries.* Chicago: ALA Editions.

Benjes-Small, Candice, Liz McGlyyn Bellamy, Jennifer Resor-Whicker, and Lisa Vassady. 2017. "Makerspace or Waste of Space: Charting a Course for Successful Academic Library Makerspaces." Paper presented at Association of College & Research Libraries Conference, Baltimore, Maryland, March 22–25, 2017. www.ala.org/acrl/sites/ala.org.acrl/files/content/conferences/confsandpreconfs/2017/MakerspaceorWasteofSpace.pdf.

"The Big6 and Super3." n.d. The Big6. https://thebig6.org/thebig6andsuper3-2.

Bray, Barbara, and Kathleen McClaskey. 2015. *Make Learning Personal: The What, Who, WOW, Where, and Why.* Thousand Oaks, CA: Corwin.

Clowes, Gavin. 2011. "The Essential 5: A Starting Point for Kagan Cooperative Learning." *Kagan Online Magazine* (Spring 2011). https://www.kaganonline.com/free_articles/research_and_rationale/330/The-Essential-5-A-Starting-Point-for-Kagan-Cooperative-Learning.

Duckworth, Angela. 2016. *Grit: The Power of Passion and Perseverance.* New York: Scribner.

Dweck, Carol S. 2006. *Mindset: the New Psychology of Success.* New York: Random House.

"Educate to Innovate." n.d. The White House. https://obamawhitehouse.archives.gov/issues/education/k-12/educate-innovate.

Eisenberg, Michael B., and Robert E. Berkowitz. 1990. *Information Problem Solving: The Big6 Skills Approach to Library and Information Skills Instruction.* Norwood, NJ: Ablex Publishing Corporation.

Fleming, Laura. 2015. *Worlds of Making: Best Practices for Establishing a Makerspace for Your School.* Thousand Oaks, CA: Corwin.

Graves, Colleen, Aaron Graves, and Diana L. Rendina. 2017. *Challenge-Based Learning in the School Library Makerspace.* Santa Barbara, CA: Libraries Unlimited.

Hasso Plattner Institute of Design at Stanford. 2010. *An Introduction to Design Thinking: Process Guide.* https://dschool- old.stanford.edu/sandbox/groups/design resources/wiki/36873/attachments/74b3d/ModeGuideBOOTCAMP2010L.pdf.

Kuhlthau, Carol. 1988. "Developing a Model of the Information Search Process of Users in Libraries." *Library and Information Science Research* 10, no. 3 (Winter 1988): 257–304.

Kuhlthau, Carol C., Leslie K. Maniotes, and Ann K. Caspari. 2012. *Guided Inquiry Design: A Framework for Inquiry in Your School.* Santa Barbara, CA: Libraries Unlimited.

Loertscher, David V., Carol Koechlin, and Sandi Zwaan. 2008. *The New Learning Commons: Where Learners Win! Reinventing School Libraries and Computer Labs.* Salt Lake City: Hi Willow Research & Publishing.

Loertscher, David V., and Carol Koechlin. 2014. "Climbing to Excellence: Defining Characteristics of Successful Learning Commons." *Knowledge Quest* 42, no. 4 (March-April): 14–15.

"Manufacturing Makerspaces." 2013. American Libraries.com (February 6, 2013). https://americanlibrariesmagazine.org/2013/02/06/manufacturing-makerspaces/.

Marzano, Robert J., Jennifer S. Norford, Michelle Finn, Douglas Finn III, Rebecca Mestaz, and Roberta Selleck. 2017. *A Handbook for Personalized Competency-Based Education.* Bloomington, IN: Marzano Research.

Moorefield-Lang, Heather. 2016. "This Is What a Maker Space Looks Like: A Visual Perspective." Presentation at American Library Association Annual Conference, Orlando, Florida., June 23–28, 2016.

Ranganathan, S. R. 1931. *The Five Laws of Library Science.* London: Edward Goldston, Ltd.

Searles, Sarah Culp. 2019. "Implementing the National School Library Standards at the District Level." *Knowledge Quest* 47, no. 5 (May-June): 50–55.

Stripling, Barbara K. 2003. "Inquiry-Based Learning." In *Curriculum Connections through the Library: Principles and Practice,* edited by Barbara K. Stripling and Sandra Hughes-Hassell, 3–39. Westport, CT: Libraries Unlimited.

About the Author

Sarah Culp Searles is supervisor of library media services for the Knox County Schools in Knoxville, Tennessee. She has served in multiple leadership roles for professional associations, including on the AASL Board of Directors and as chair of the *Knowledge Quest* editorial board. Sarah is a Lilead Fellow and in 2018 was named a distinguished administrator by the Tennessee Association of School Librarians. She is a frequent speaker and professional development facilitator at the local, state, and national levels, especially on topics related to school library instruction, collaboration, and leadership. Her articles on school libraries have been published in *Knowledge Quest* and *School Library Connection*.

Index

An italicized page number indicates an illustration or table.

D

SHARED FOUNDATIONS

Explore

SHARED FOUNDATIONS SERIES

I. **INQUIRE,** by Lori Donovan

II. **INCLUDE,** by Julie Stivers

III. **COLLABORATE,** by Mary Catherine Coleman

IV. **CURATE,** by Len Bryan and Daniella Smith

V. **EXPLORE,** by Sarah Culp Searles

VI. **ENGAGE,** by Kathryn Roots Lewis and Marcia A. Mardis